Discovering
Scottish
Writers

Edited by
Alan Reid
and
Brian D. Osborne

Scottish Library Association
and
Scottish Cultural Press

ISBN 1 898218 84 6

Designed by GSB, Edinburgh

The publishers acknowledge subsidy from the Scottish Arts Council
towards the publication of this volume.

Scottish Library Association
Scottish Centre for Information & Library Services
1 John Street
Hamilton ML3 7EU

Scottish Cultural Press
Leith Walk Business Centre
130 Leith Walk
Edinburgh EH6 5DT

Introduction

Scottish literature has had a major impact on the shaping of Scottish culture and on Scottish national identity. **Discovering Scottish Writers** fills a distinct gap in the coverage of the literature of Scotland. Aimed at the general reader and the student **Discovering Scottish Writers** combines authority with accessibility, scholarship with enthusiasm.

Eighty of the greatest Scottish literary figures of the past, ranging in time from John Barbour in the fourteenth to Jessie Kesson in the twentieth century, are discussed and set in their context by a specially selected group of academics and enthusiasts. The contributors have been asked to conform to a standard length and style of entry and to discuss their subject's life, place in Scottish literature and main works - where appropriate, quotations from works have been included. Information has been provided on monuments, memorials and sites associated with the writers in the hope that **Discovering Scottish Writers** might be useful for the tourist and visitor. The involvement of the Scottish Library Association in this project and the presence of a number of librarians as contributors reflects the wealth of material available on these and other writers in libraries, and in particular in local studies collections, throughout the country.

While a uniform approach has been adopted we are sure that both the character of the subject and the personality of the contributor will become very clear to the reader and that the authority and variety of the contributors will add interest and pleasure to the book's undoubted value as a work of reference and information.

The choice of authors to include in such a work is always going to be a controversial matter and the editors have compounded this by arbitrarily determining that ten of their eighty great writers are pre-eminently distinguished and merit extended treatment in 1000 words over two pages. The remaining seventy are dealt with in 500 words on one page. While there is unlikely to be controversy about the central core of authors in the Scottish canon there is much scope for argument and debate about the selection and de-selection of some of the more marginal writers. One factor that we have taken into account in making our selection was that, all other things being equal, we would prefer to include writers whose works were readily available and in print. We have also, for reasons of length, chiefly confined ourselves to writers of imaginative literature, acknowledging that by doing so we lose some very distinctive Scottish voices such as Adam Smith and David Hume. A further basis for selection, it must be confessed was editorial prejudice and enthusiasm.

We would like to take this opportunity to express our thanks to all the contributors for their support for this project, for their willing acceptance of a very prescriptive and demanding editorial brief and for their ability to communicate their knowledge and delight for their subject to a wide general audience.

Alan Reid • Brian D. Osborne

Alasdair MacMhaighstir Alasdair

Poet

Arisaig Graveyard

Alasdair MacMhaighstir Alasdair (Alasdair Macdonald) was born about 1695 in Ardnamurchan where his father, a near relative of Clanranald, was an Episcopalian minister. He received a good education and is said to have studied at Glasgow University. In 1729 he was appointed by the Society for the Propagation of Christian Knowledge as teacher of a Charity School at Island Finnan, and he continued in this and other centres for about fifteen years. With his duties as schoolmaster he combined the office of Catechist, an office to which he was appointed by the Presbytery of Mull.

Sometime in the '40s he turned Catholic and became an enthusiastic propagandist for Prince Charles in whose army he served as a captain, fought in various campaigns and was on the march to Derby. He wrote a number of passionate Jacobite songs, one with the refrain:

O hi ri ri he is coming
o hi ri ri our exiled king
Let us take our arms and clothing
and the flowing tartan plaid

He also of course wrote other poems not connected with the '45. His **Oran an t-Samhraidh** (Song of Summer) has a wonderful freshness with which Duncan Ban Macintyre may have been competing in his own poem of the same title. He also wrote **Oran a Gheamhraidh** (Song of Winter). He had a wonderful range of vocabulary and splendid distinctive detail.

However the poem for which he is most famous (as Duncan Ban Macintyre for **Ben Doran**) is the **Birlinn** (or Galley) **of Clanranald**. In this poem there is detailed description of the leading seamen some of whom may have been historical persons. There is a lot of technical detail. The poem begins with A Blessing of the Ship, followed by a Blessing of the Arms. Then there is an Incitement to Rowing to the Sailing Point. There are sixteen men seated at the oars. Perhaps the most dramatic (even melodramatic) part of the poem is the storm in which the sea is disturbed to an extraordinary extent:

The whole sea turned to porridge
foul and turbid
with the blood and filth of splayed sea-beasts
turned red and horrid

The poem with its detail and drama is one of the major poems in Gaelic and if Duncan Ban Macintyre wrote of glens and the deer, Macdonald wrote of seamen and the sea and a tremendous storm in equally fine detail.

During the last twenty years of his life Macdonald lived in Glenuig, Knoydart, Morar and Arisaig. He died about the year 1770 and is buried at Arisaig.

A translation of the storm scene from the **Birlinn** can be found in Iain Crichton Smith's **Collected Poems** (Carcanet 1992). A number of Macdonald's poems including **Song of Summer**, **Song of Winter** and some of his Jacobite songs can be found translated in Professor Derick Thomson's **Gaelic Poetry in the Eighteenth Century - a Bilingual Anthology** (The Association for Scottish Literary Studies 1993).

Iain Crichton Smith

William Alexander

William Alexander

Novelist, social historian & journalist

Alexander was born on 12th June 1826 at the farm of Westerhouses, Rescivet, in the Garioch, the first son of Anne Wilson of Old Rayne and James Alexander whose family had been tenant farmers in Aberdeenshire since the seventeenth century. His career as a farmer ended at the age of twenty, when a serious accident led to the loss of a leg. Through membership of the Mutual Instruction Union he met the writer William McCombie and in 1852 became the reporter on his newspaper, the **North of Scotland Gazette**, shortly afterwards retitled the **Aberdeen Free Press**.

Alexander's novel **Johnny Gibb of Gushetneuk**, begun as a serial in the **Free Press** on 28th September 1869, won fame as a classic of vernacular Scots. It was re-published in book form in 1871 and has seldom been out of print since.

But Alexander shunned self-publicity so effectively that the full extent of his writing has only recently been appreciated. This includes five further novels which were published as serials in his own paper between 1852 and 1877, including **The Laird of Drammochdyle**, **Ravenshowe and the Residenters Therein**, and **My Uncle The Baillie**. These discoveries establish **Johnny Gibb** as the central novel in an epic sequence covering more than a century of social and economic change.

Alexander abandoned standard literary Scots in favour of demotic spoken forms, and his political outlook was similarly radical. He tackled the burning issues of the day — exploitation of the workers, unemployment, public health, the evils of landlordism and corruption in local government. In **My Uncle The Baillie**, a young apprentice is quizzed about his prospects in an obviously venal environment:

> *We're jist settin' on to hatch a new brodmill o' toon cooncillors … but ye've nae public spirit ava; fat greater object o' public ambition can be set afore an aspirin' youth than to busy 'imsel' i' the toon's affairs, win into the Coonicl, takin' fat share he can get o' the scran, an', feenally sit doon wi' a baillie's chyne aneth's chowks?*

His work demonstrates the presence of a sophisticated literary realism in a tradition previously dismissed as having dwindled into Kailyard sentimentality. It is central to the revaluation of nineteenth century Scottish literature now taking place.

William Alexander became editor of the **Free Press** in 1870, and later vice-president of the Institute of Journalists. He was a Council member of the New Spalding Club and the Aberdeen Philosophical Society, and was active in many projects for the benefit of the City. In 1886 he was awarded an LLD by the University of Aberdeen. He died in Aberdeen on 19th February, 1894, and is commemorated by a handsome monument in Nellfield Cemetery.

William Alexander, **Johnnie Gibb of Gushetneuk**, Tuckwell, 1995.
William Alexander, **My Uncle The Baillie**, Tuckwell, 1995.
William Alexander, **Rural Life in Victorian Aberdeenshire**, Mercat, 1992.
William Alexander, **The Laird of Drammochdyle**, AUP, 1986.
William Donaldson, **Popular Literature in Victorian Scotland: Language Fiction and the Press**, AUP, 1986.

William Donaldson

Marion Angus

Poet

Marion Angus was born in 1866 in Aberdeen. Her childhood was spent in Arbroath, where her father was a minister of the United Presbyterian Kirk. After his death, Angus moved to Aberdeen, living much of her adult life there with her sister and mother (who came from the Borders). Her poetry, mainly in Angus Scots, ranges around the north east of Scotland, what Angus herself calls "the cauld east countra" in her poem, **Gathering Shells**. Marion Angus was an early member of Scottish PEN. She died in 1946, in Arbroath.

Marion Angus contributed poetry and stories to journals when quite young, but began writing seriously later in life. Her work was published in Hugh MacDiarmid's **Northern Numbers** (1921-2), and in **The Lilt and Other Poems** (1922), **The Tinker's Road** (1924), **Sun and Candlelight** (1927), **The Singin' Lass** (1929), **The Turn of the Day** (1931), **Lost Country and Other Verses** (1937). A **Selected Poems** was edited by Maurice Lindsay (1950), and contains a personal memoir by Helen Cruickshank. Angus's poems are influenced by the ballads and Scottish folk song. Generally short and deceptively simple, they are spare and elliptic; while sometimes described as "fey", at their best they are powerful and disturbing.

Marion Angus

Characteristically compressed is **The Turn of the Day**. The opening suggests the coming of new life and hope:

> *Under the cauld, green grass*
> *I hear the waukenin' burn*

But the speaker, paradoxically, does not welcome spring. This poem, like much of Angus's work, subtly subverts reader expectations, and suggests strong emotions, loss and grief. Much of her poetry deals with disappointment or love denied, and with death and mortality. Compassion and a tenderness for the poor and excluded are implied, too, as in **The Wild Lass** and **Welcome**, in a world often characterised by Angus as wintry and menacing.

Dorothy Porter in **Cencrastus,** Spring 1987 writes of Angus's "covert narratives" in poems which often suggest "secret stories", as in the disquieting **The Blue Jacket** and **The Can'el**. Although Angus creates voices both male and female, her subjects are most often women, such as **Jean Cam'bell**, or the independent woman speaking in **Invitation**:

> *Luve, come clasp me*
> *Whaur the twa burns rin, -*
> *A' but the white soul o' me*
> *That ye can never win.*

Places are important in her work, too, often suggesting a sense of "otherness" (as in **The Tinker's Road**, and **The Seaward Toon**), of the numinous, and sometimes of menace and unease. There is a brooding, as well, on the Scottish past and tradition in poems like **The Fiddler** and **Remembrance Day.**

Marion Angus wrote some fine English poems, including **Alas! Poor Queen** and **Anemones**, but her work in Scots is especially significant, not only for the development of later poets, but as an achievement in its own right.

Carol Anderson

R M Ballantyne

R M Ballantyne

Writer of boys' adventure novels

Robert Michael Ballantyne was born at 25 Ann Street, Edinburgh on 24th April 1825, the son of Alexander Thomson Ballantyne. His uncles James and John Ballantyne were involved with Archibald Constable in the publishing of Sir Walter Scott's novels and the family was ruined financially by the crash of the business in 1826.

Following his education at the Edinburgh Academy Ballantyne entered the service of the Hudson's Bay Company and between 1841 and 1847 worked with them as a clerk at the Red River Settlement in Canada. The experience was to provide him with the background for his first adventure tale for young people, **The Young Fur Traders** which followed the adventures of a young man called Charles Kennedy. Published in 1856, it was a loosely autobiographical account of Ballantyne's own time with the Hudson's Bay Company in Canada and its success prompted a series of adventure stories set at sea or in the American west and the jungles of Africa. Between then and his death in 1894 Ballantyne published some eighty novels which echoed the Victorian enthusiasm for the ideals of service to the British empire. The best known of these is **Coral Island** (1858) which tells the gripping story of three young castaways on a Pacific island - the narrator Ralph and his friends Jack Martin and Peterkin Gay. Like Robinson Crusoe they have to make do with bare essentials and endure many adventures, including a fight with cannibals, before they are rescued. Also worthy of note are **Martin Rattler** (1859), **The Dog Crusoe** (1861), **The Gorilla Hunters** (1862) and **Black Ivory** (1873).

Together with contemporaries such as G.A. Henty, Michael Fenn and W.H.G. Kingston, Ballantyne became a regular contributor to the **Boy's Own Paper** which produced patriotic adventure stories set in the remote parts of the empire. Through his prodigious output Ballantyne quickly became one of the best known and best paid adventure writers of his day. Freed from the need to earn a living - in 1848 he had returned to Edinburgh to support his mother and five sisters by working as clerk with the North British Railway Company - Ballantyne was able to travel widely to research the backgrounds for his novels. His latter years were spent in France and England and he died in Rome on 8th February 1894. During his time in Edinburgh Ballantyne lived at 6 Millerfield Place near the Meadows and was a regular attender at the nearby Chalmers Memorial Church.

During his lifetime he enjoyed widespread popularity for his ability to produce credible adventures in vividly realised settings. Much influenced by Scott, Ballantyne was able to create heroes who are romantic and chivalric ideals of manhood and their adventures are pictured as glorious and fulfilling deeds of derring-do. However, as interest in the empire began to wane after the First World War so too did Ballantyne's novels lose their appeal and in time they became little more than literary curiosities.

Trevor Royle

John Barbour

Poet

John Barbour (c.1320-1395), commonly termed "the father of Scottish literature", was author of **The Bruce**, the earliest Scottish poem of any length that is now extant. Nothing is known of Barbour's early life, but in 1357 he became Archdeacon of Aberdeen, an office that he held till his death in 1395. As archdeacon he was second in rank only to the bishop of his diocese, and conducted ecclesiastical courts concerning arrears in teinds (tithes), and other offences. There is no evidence that Barbour possessed a university degree, but most archdeacons had a knowledge of canon and civil law; he seems to have studied for a short time in Oxford, and on other occasions travelled, on pilgrimage or for study, in England and France. Barbour was an Auditor of the Exchequer to Robert II, and received from him a pension and other payments, apparently in recognition of his literary labours.

Barbour wrote a lost genealogical work, **The Stewartis Originall**, and modern scholars have attributed other poems to him. But the only work that is certainly his is **The Bruce** (usually dated to the late 1370s), which celebrates Robert Bruce (Robert I) and the War of Independence. Barbour himself called the poem a "romance", and was clearly familiar with the chivalric themes and stories popular in the Middle Ages: he depicts Bruce as reading aloud the romance of **Fierabras** to his troops, while they were waiting to cross Loch Lomond. But from the outset Barbour stresses his concern with "suthfastnes", or truth, and the poem is largely faithful to historical fact, much more so than Blind Harry's **Wallace**. Nonetheless the portrait of Bruce is idealized, and the history is exemplary, designed to instruct Barbour's contemporaries at a period when Scotland was split into factions. A passage in praise of freedom is justly famous:

> A! fredome is a noble thing!
> Fredome mays [makes] man to haif liking [delight];
> Fredome all solace to man giffis:
> He levys [lives] at ese that frely levys.   (I. 225-8)

But Barbour also celebrates other values - "treuthe", or personal loyalty, courage in adversity, and, above all, the strong and effective leadership that is embodied in Bruce, his model of a good king.

Barbour is a competent story-teller, although his octosyllabic couplets are occasionally monotonous. His style is swift, laconic, and colloquial; yet he is not lacking in rhetorical art, and set-pieces of portraiture and oratory, such as Bruce's speech at Bannockburn, are interspersed among the vivid accounts of sieges, battles and single combat.

Barbour's Bruce, ed. Matthew P. McDiarmid and J. A. C. Stevenson, 3 vols. Scottish Text Society, Edinburgh, 1980-85.

Selections from books I, II, and XII, in **Longer Scottish Poems: I 1375-1650**, ed. Priscilla Bawcutt and Felicity Riddy, Edinburgh, 1987.

Lois Ebin, John Barbour's **Bruce**: Poetry, History and Propaganda in **Studies in Scottish Literature**, 9 1972, 218-42.

R. James Goldstein, **The Matter of Scotland: Historical Narrative in Medieval Scotland**, University of Nebraska Press, Lincoln and London, 1993.

Priscilla Bawcutt

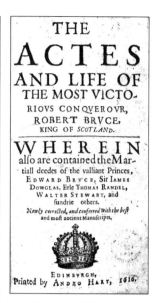

THE
ACTES
AND LIFE OF
THE MOST VICTO-
RIOVS CONQVEROVR,
ROBERT BRVCE,
KING OF SCOTLAND.

WHEREIN
alſo are contained the Mar-
tiall deedes of the valliant Princes,
EDWARD BRVCE, Sir IAMES
DOWGLAS, Erle THOMAS RANDEL,
WALTER STEWART, and
ſundrie others.
Newly corrected, and conferred with the beſt
and moſt ancient Manuſcripts.

EDINBVRGH,
Printed by ANDRO HART, 1616.

"The Bruce" title page, 1616.

James Barke

Novelist

James Barke

James Barke was born in 1905 at Torwoodlee, Selkirkshire, the son of farmworkers from Galloway who moved to Tulliallan, Fife when he was two. A gritty, unsentimental account of his childhood appeared in his autobiography **The Green Hills Far Away** (1940). In 1918 the Barkes moved to Glasgow. Although his original ambition was to become an engineer, James became a cost accountant with the Clyde shipbuilders, Barclay Curle.

In 1933 he published his first novel **The World is his Pillow** which enjoyed a moderate success and encouraged him to persevere. **The Wild Macraes** (1934) was even more popular. Two years later, with the success of **Major Operation**, Barke decided to retire from the shipyard and devote his time wholly to writing. Other books followed in quick succession: **Gregarach, The End of the High Bridge** and **The Devil in his Kitchen**.

Land of the Leal appeared in 1939 and traced the saga of Jean and David Ramsay and their lifelong quest for peace of mind, set against a graphic picture of Scottish life in the late nineteenth and early twentieth centuries. Their son Andy, the shipyard worker, was Barke himself. In painting this picture, Barke drew heavily on observation of his own parents. Against a background of social upheaval young David Ramsay decides that there is something better in life than the unremitting harshness and brutality of a Galloway farm.

This was undoubtedly Barke's best book, and the one which made his most important and lasting contribution to Scottish literature, comparable in scope and design to Lewis Grassic Gibbon's **A Scots Quair**. It also gave Barke the appellation of a Marxist, although if he were to have accepted any label it would have been a Scottish Nationalist. A profound love of all things Scottish led him to Burns, especially during the Second World War when he was compelled to return to Barclay Curle as an alternative to military service. During the war years he conceived what he hoped would be his masterpiece, a trilogy entitled **Immortal Memory** telling the story of Robert Burns. The three volumes, beginning in 1946 with **The Wind that Shakes the Barley**, eventually stretched to five by 1954. The following year he produced an edition of the poems and songs of Burns which claimed sixty previously unpublished works; this edition is still in print although it was roundly condemned by critics at the time and has muddied the waters of Burns scholarship ever since.

With the financial security of the Burns novels, Barke and his wife Nan moved from Bearsden to Daljarrock, Ayrshire which they ran as a hotel for some years. Sadly, Barke became an alcoholic, lost his estate and latterly moved back to Glasgow where he died suddenly in 1958. A sixth novel on the Burns theme, **Bonnie Jean**, appeared posthumously in 1959. Barke also collaborated with DeLancey Ferguson and Sidney Goodsir Smith on an edition of the **Merry Muses of Caledonia**, as well as writing a number of wartime three-act plays with a strong social theme.

James Mackay

Sir J M Barrie

Novelist & dramatist.

James Matthew Barrie was born in Kirriemuir (Forfarshire), the "Thrums" of his fiction, on 9th May 1860, the seventh surviving child of a hand-loom weaver. Educated at Glasgow Academy, Forfar Academy and Dumfries Academy, he took his MA at Edinburgh University. He worked as a journalist for the **Nottingham Journal** before moving to London in 1885 to freelance. Success came with a series of sketches of life in bygone Thrums contributed to the **St. James's Gazette**, published in 1888 as **Auld Licht Idylls**, followed by **When a Man's Single** (1888) and **A Window in Thrums** (1889). These works and the novels **The Little Minister** (1891), **Sentimental Tommy** (1896) and its sequel **Tommy and Grizel** (1900) have been regarded by George Blake and others as examples of the Kailyard School. Leonee Ormond's **J. M. Barrie** (1987) argues that it is more rewarding to assess Barrie's regional fiction beside that of Hardy and George Eliot.

Sir J M Barrie

Barrie's dramatised adaptation of **The Little Minister** was enormously successful, persuading him to write increasingly for the stage. Notable among his early plays are **Quality Street** (1902), **The Admirable Crichton** (1902) and **What Every Woman Knows** (1908). In 1894 he married the actress Mary Ansell. The marriage was childless and ended in divorce in 1909. However, he had befriended and was ultimately to adopt the five boys of Arthur and Sylvia Llewelyn Davies, a relationship brilliantly explored in Andrew Birkin's book, **J. M. Barrie and the Lost Boys** (1979). Out of stories he spun for the Davies boys came the material for **Peter Pan** (1904), probably the most famous children's play ever written. It is a complex work, perceptive and unsentimental about childhood. Peter, "the boy who would not grow up", the conceited leader of the Lost Boys of Never Land, forever dodges the world of adulthood. Like Sherlock Holmes he seems destined for greater immortality than his creator.

Honours followed - a baronetcy in 1913, the Order of Merit in 1922, the Rectorship of St. Andrews University, to whom he delivered a moving address on **Courage** (1922), and the Chancellorship of Edinburgh University. His later plays include **Dear Brutus** (1917), **Mary Rose** (1920), and **The Boy David** (1936). A final work of fiction, the ghost-story **Farewell Miss Julie Logan**, appeared in **The Times** in 1931. Barrie died on 19th June, 1937.

Despite the celebrity attaching to Barrie thanks to **Peter Pan**, there has been scant critical interest in the remainder of his prolific output, in particular his essays and letters, although R. D. S. Jack's **The Road to the Never Land** (1991) persuasively describes his genius for stagecraft.

Barrie's grave is in Kirriemuir Cemetery, and his birthplace at 4, Brechin Road is maintained as a museum by The National Trust for Scotland. Many of the localities in his fiction may still be identified in Kirriemuir. A statue of Peter Pan stands in the town square, a smaller version of that in London's Hyde Park, and a pavilion housing a camera obscura which he gifted to the town in 1930 on being made its only Freeman.

John MacRitchie

George Blake

George Blake

Novelist

George Blake was born in Greenock on 28th October 1893. He was educated at Greenock Academy, then at Glasgow University where World War I interrupted his legal studies. He was wounded at Gallipoli and wrote **The Path to Glory** about his experiences. After the War he took up journalism, working for the **Glasgow Evening News** under Neil Munro's editorship, later editing selections of Munro's journalism, **The Brave Days** and **The Looker-On**. Blake's first novel **The Vagabond Papers** was published in 1922. In 1923, he married Ellie Malcolm Lawson with whom he had two sons and a daughter. In 1924 he became acting editor of **John O'London's Weekly** and in 1928 moved to **Strand Magazine** but was unable to restore its fortunes. In 1930 he became a director of the Porpoise Press, an imprint of Faber and Faber. The Porpoise Press was established to stimulate and publish Scottish writing, interest in which was high at the time. Of the writers linked with the Scottish Literary Renaissance Neil Gunn probably had the closest links with Porpoise. Apart from a period in World War II when Blake worked for the Ministry of Information he lived in Scotland from 1932 onwards.

Blake was a familiar figure on the Scottish literary scene. His analysis of the literature of the 1920s and '30s is contained in **Barrie and the Kailyard School** (1951) and **Annals of Scotland 1895-1955: An Essay on the Twentieth Century Scottish Novel** (1956) written to supplement a series of BBC radio broadcasts. Blake reflects on the popular fiction of the Kailyard, acknowledging some merit in it, but seeing in its easy sentimentalism "a betrayal of the realities of Scottish life". Although Blake praises Lewis Grassic Gibbon's description of rural life in **Sunset Song** as "farming with the gloves off'', he was convinced that the Kailyard had deflected attention from the life of the urban working class. In order to redress this imbalance he wrote **The Shipbuilders** (1935) which described the contrasting lives of a shipyard owner and a riveter. Of this programmatic novel Blake later wrote that he pled "guilty to an insufficient knowledge of working class life and to the adoption of a middle-class attitude to the theme of industrial conflict and despair''. Blake's vision was not always commensurate with his literary ability but this attempt at a proletarian novel stands as an early example of what has become a fine tradition of Scottish writing in the fiction of Edward Gaitens, Robin Jenkins, William McIlvanney and James Kelman. Blake's fiction is more successful in the "Garvel" novels which are set in Greenock and follow the lives of sailors, ship designers, ship builders and their families. **The Westering Sun** (1946) and **The Constant Star** (1946) demonstrate this love of the Clyde and its ships.

Not all Blake's output was concerned with literary matters. He wrote industrial histories of the British India Shipping Company and Lloyd's Register of Shipping as well as contributing a volume, **The Trials of Patrick Carraher**, to Notable British Trials. He continued to write for the **Scottish Daily Express** and the **Glasgow Herald** until the end of his life. He died on 30th August 1961.

Beth Dickson

James Boswell

Biographer, diarist & travel writer

James Boswell

Boswell was born in Edinburgh on 29th October 1740, the eldest son of Alexander and Euphemia Boswell. His father was an Ayrshire laird and advocate who, on appointment to the Court of Session in 1754, took the judicial title of Lord Auchinleck.

Boswell studied at Edinburgh and Glasgow Universities, his father intending him for a career as an advocate, although his own ambitions were for a literary or a military career. He ran off to London in 1760 and was received into the Roman Catholic church. He was persuaded that this conversion, which would have precluded public office or professional advancement, was unwise and after a taste of the wilder side of London life returned home to his studies and continuing tension with his father. Eventually, in 1762, he was permitted to pay an extended visit to London, where he made full use of his freedom, overindulging in drink and sex. However in Davies's bookshop in May 1763 he met the man who was to become the central figure in his life - Samuel Johnson. Their opening conversation was unpromising:

> Boswell: "Mr Johnson, indeed I come from Scotland, but I cannot help it."
> Johnson: "Sir, that, I find, is what a very great many of your countrymen cannot help."

In 1763 Boswell was sent to study law at Utrecht and then travelled widely on the Continent, meeting Voltaire and Rousseau, introducing himself as:

> a Scots gentleman of ancient family

He visited Corsica, meeting the Corsican leader General Paoli. In 1768 he published **An Account of Corsica** (1768) which won him an international reputation. His legal career progressed satisfactorily although he was torn between the attractions of London and his attachment to Scotland:

> I have a kind of idea of Scottish patriotism that makes me think it a duty to spend my money in my own country

In 1773 he and Johnson made an extensive tour of the Scottish Highlands. Both men wrote accounts of this journey, Boswell's **Journal of a Tour to the Hebrides** appearing in 1784. Between 1777 and 1783 he contributed to the **London Magazine**. In 1791 he published his masterpiece - the **Life of Samuel Johnson**, generally considered as the greatest English-language biography .

In 1769 Boswell married his cousin, Margaret Montgomerie, had six children, and succeeded to the family estate in 1782. He was called to the English Bar in 1786 and settled in London. He died in London on 19th May 1795 and is buried in the family vault at Auchinleck.

Boswell's reputation, until this century, was as Johnson's biographer and he is often dismissed as being simply the Doctor's sycophantic disciple. Boswell's difficult relationship with Alexander Boswell probably resulted in Johnson becoming a father-figure, but his portrayal of Johnson in the **Tour** and the **Life** is well-rounded and objective. The modern publication of Boswell's diaries, remarkable for their scope, self-awareness and frankness, revealed a fascinatingly complex character and placed Boswell among the great diarists and auto-biographers.

Brian D. Osborne

James Bridie

James Bridie

Dramatist

Bridie was born Osborne Henry Mavor in Glasgow on 3rd January 1888. He studied medicine at Glasgow University, qualifying in 1913. During the 1914-18 War he served in the RAMC in the Middle East. He then pursued a medical career, but his passion for the theatre gradually took over and his last ten years were spent solely as a professional dramatist. He died in 1951, the founding father of modern Scottish theatre.

His first play, **The Switchback**, about a doctor tempted by fame and wealth, was written in 1922 but not performed until 1929. His range was wide: plays medical **A Sleeping Clergyman**, (1933), biblical **Tobias and the Angel**, (1930), Scottish **Mr Bolfry**, (1943), experimental **Daphne Laureola**, (1949).

Bridie is often described as a follower of Shaw in his delight in ideas and debate, but Bridie is never less than interested in people - it is fallible human beings arguing that he loves - a very Scottish trait. He had a gift for dialogue and the retelling of old stories. His work is characterised by a celebration of the human spirit, its mixture of "dirt and deity", the opposition of appearance and reality, the deflation of pretension, the investigation of moral dilemmas - presented with irony, wit and a serious levity. These qualities are evident in one of his best plays, **The Anatomist** (1930), based on events in the life of Dr Robert Knox, the nineteenth century Edinburgh anatomist who was supplied with bodies for dissection by the notorious Burke and Hare. Knox is played as a theatrical dandy - a "barnstormer" - but dedicated to medical research, even if it means implication in murder. He is an ambiguous character; there is a worrying glamour about this justifier of the means justifying the end. Knox accepts this and the consequences:

> *Do you think because I strut and rant and put on a bold face that my soul isn't sick within me at the horror of what I have done?... No, I carry the deaths of these poor wretches round my neck till I die ...*

A major criticism has been Bridie's apparent inability to resolve his plays. To some extent this is the case, but Bridie retorted:

> *Only God can write last acts, and He seldom does. You should go out of the theatre with your head whirling with speculations.*
> **One Way of Living**, (1939)

Bridie pretended to be indolent and retiring. He was actually a workaholic. In addition to writing over forty plays he was actively involved in founding Glasgow Citizens' Theatre in 1943 and in 1950 the first College of Drama in Scotland. In his day he was highly successful with most of his plays premiered in London. They are rarely seen now. Only **The Anatomist** and **Tobias** are in print. It is surely time for a revival - his work is humorous, vigorous, stimulating and, above all, entertaining. Bridie had no successor in his style, but perhaps echoes of his whimsical arguments about Life, Death and Art can be heard in the work of Alasdair Gray.

Hamish Whyte

George Douglas Brown

Novelist

George Douglas Brown

George Douglas Brown, who sometimes wrote under the pen names "Kennedy King" and "George Douglas", was born on 26th January 1869 in Ochiltree, Ayrshire to George Douglas Brown, a farmer, and Sarah Gemmell, a farm-servant of Irish descent; Brown was illegitimate. He was educated at local schools in Ochiltree and Coylton, attending Ayr Academy from 1883. From 1887-1890 he studied at the University of Glasgow, taking a First in Classics and in 1891 he won a scholarship to Balliol College, Oxford. Although maintaining his academic record, he did not enjoy Oxford, feeling that he did not fit in socially. Before he was due to sit his final examinations, he returned to Ayrshire to nurse his mother in her last illness; the consequent mixture of stress and grief contributed to his taking only a third class degree in the examinations of 1895.

Brown settled in London and made his living by journalism and teaching. In 1899 he published **Love and a Sword** under the pen name "Kennedy King". He contributed a mixture of short fictions and critical articles to various journals including **Blackwood's Magazine** and also "read" for the publisher John MacQueen. In the autumn of 1900 he began writing the book for which he became famous **The House with the Green Shutters**. Brown's health failed in 1902 and he died at the London home of his friend Andrew Melrose. He was buried in Ayr, beside his mother.

When it was published in 1901, **The House with the Green Shutters** was acclaimed by critics as a counterblast to the current fashion for "Kailyard fiction", popular fiction which dealt in stereotypes of Scottish rural life showing small communities working together with wit and homely wisdom to overcome life's difficulties. By contrast, Brown's small community, Barbie, based on Ochiltree, is a nest of jealousy and spite, often expressed in the "barbed" comments of the "bodies", local gossips. They are resentful of Gourlay's success which comes from his carting business and has brought him his great prize, his house with the green shutters. Gourlay, domineering and brutish, is not commercially acute enough to change his business methods as industrialisation begins to affect Ayrshire. After some damaging setbacks, Gourlay sends his son to University to train him for a safe professional position which will restore the family fortunes. Though gifted, young John Gourlay is temperamentally unstable. He slides into alcoholism, returns to Barbie in disgrace and provoked by the "bodies" murders his father in a fit of drunken resentment. John, his mother and sister, then take their own lives.

Because of its unsentimental portrayal of Scottish life, **The House with the Green Shutters** was championed by emerging Scottish Modernists, such as Hugh MacDiarmid, Lewis Grassic Gibbon and Neil Gunn. Later critics have noted in the harsh, laconic character of John Gourlay and the demonic images in which he is sometimes cast, close links with the work of Robert Burns, Walter Scott, James Hogg and Robert Louis Stevenson while the work's superbly fluent Scots is reminiscent of John Galt, a writer Brown greatly admired.

Beth Dickson

John Buchan

Novelist, publisher & politician

John Buchan

Buchan was born on 26th August 1875 in Perth, son of a Free Church of Scotland minister, later domiciled in Glasgow and Peebles. Like his sister Anna (1877-1948) the popular novelist "O. Douglas", he was educated at Hutcheson's Grammar School, Glasgow. At Glasgow University Buchan produced an anthology of Bacon's essays, and a novel deriving from Conan Doyle's recent Brigadier Gerard stories, blended with the Borders and their Covenant legends he knew so well, **Sir Quixote of the Moors**. Thence he went to Oxford which made him take another first degree as though Glasgow could not award one.

Buchan's acquiescence in this dishonour to his country of origin, and the first laurels it had given him, symbolised the dilemma of his literary life. The English establishment received his deference and gave him rewards, but Scotland provided both his richest sources and his bedrock of reassurance. His devotion to Scott and Stevenson would repay itself with historical novels such as **John Burnet of Barns** (1898), and **Witch Wood** (1927), both showing their sense of Scots divided loyalties. Buchan spoke to his less fortunate counterparts through popular anthologies and biographies of writers such as Izaak Walton, Edmund Burke, Walter Scott, Walter Raleigh, Montrose, Julius Caesar and - less literary - Augustus and Cromwell.

But Buchan's greatest literary triumphs reveal his own insecurity as to his conquest of and by England. The terror of the young lawyer suddenly surrounded by agents of an establishment intent on his destruction (**The Power House**); the alienated South African fleeing to a womb-like Scotland pursued by police and enemy spies (**The Thirty-Nine Steps** and, with transfer to a German setting, **Greenmantle**); the dream of Scottish fortune colliding with the vision of a liberated black Africa (**Prester John**); new ideals in the promise of slum Scottish schoolboys (**Huntingtower**); the fascination of landed and moneyed success briefly (and fraudulently) risking all in a wild outlaw adventure (**John Macnab**); the early ethnic rivalry implicit in his anti-Semitic flashes being replaced by a celebration of Jewish integrity culminating in the death of the hero at the hands of Nazis (**A Prince of the Captivity**, 1933, almost certainly the first major anti-Nazi popular novel).

Buchan crowned his political career as Baron Tweedsmuir, Governor-General of Canada (1935-40) and Chancellor of Edinburgh University; and he crowned his literary career with the posthumous **Sick Heart River**, virtually describing his own dying in the metaphor of his hero Leithen giving his last months to the aid of doomed Indians. A Catholic priest obituarises Leithen:

> *His noble, frosty egoism was merged in something nobler. He had meant to die in the cold cathedral of the North, ceasing to live in a world which had no care for life. Now he welcomed the humblest human environment, for he had come to love his kind, indeed, to love everything that God had made.*

Buchan died in Canada on 11th February 1940, almost exactly on the date he evidently intended for the passing of Leithen.

Owen Dudley Edwards

Robert Burns

Poet

Robert Burns

Burns was born at Alloway near Ayr on 25th January 1759, the eldest of a family of seven born to William and Agnes Burnes. The Burnes family hailed from Kincardineshire, but William had moved south in the aftermath of the Jacobite rebellion, first to Edinburgh and then to Ayrshire where he was employed as a landscape gardener. In 1757 he married Agnes Brown whose family had lived in the Kirkoswald and Maybole district for generations.

The future poet's earliest years were spent in the "auld cley biggin", the cottage which William Burnes had erected on a portion of the land which he had feued as a market garden, and it was here that he and his brother Gilbert received their brief formal education at the hands of John Murdoch. In 1765 the family moved to Mount Oliphant, a 70-acre farm two miles away. It was here, in the autumn of 1774, that Burns wrote his first song **Handsome Nell** as a tribute to the girl with whom he was partnered at harvest-time. With the exception of the **Tragic Fragment** (in blank verse), all of Burns's early compositions were lyrics set to well-known melodies of the period, and song writing was to be his principal metier till the end of his life.

At Whitsun 1777 the Burnes family moved to Lochlie, a hill farm of 130 acres in Tarbolton parish. Three years later Burns took a leading part in founding the Tarbolton Bachelors' Club, a convivial debating society widely regarded as the prototype for the many Burns clubs now flourishing worldwide. In 1780 he was inducted into the local masonic lodge; freemasonery was to be a major influence on his life, and helped launch his literary career

William Burnes died in February 1784, broken by prolonged litigation over the lease of Lochlie. The following month Robert and Gilbert decided to alter the spelling of their surname, and about that time took the lease of Mossgiel farm near Mauchline. The death of William Burnes had a liberating influence on Robert; 1784 was his *annus mirabilis* and a great deal of the poetry which would appear in his first edition was composed in this brief period.

He was liberated in other ways also, with unfortunate results. In 1785 Elizabeth Paton, a farm-servant, gave birth to a daughter. Characteristically Burns celebrated the event in verses which he pithily entitled **A Poet's Welcome to a Bastart Wean**. By now Rab Mossgiel was acquiring a reputation (in two or three parishes) as a versifier and wit. An affair with Jean Armour, a master-mason's daughter, had inevitable results. Hounded by the girl's father, Burns had a brief affair with a byrewoman at Coilsfield, Margaret 'Highland Mary' Campbell, which ended tragically with her death from typhoid fever which may have been exacerbated by pregnancy.

Deciding to emigrate to Jamaica, Burns cast about for some way of raising the £20 to pay his fare, and decided to publish his poems. **Poems, Chiefly in the Scottish Dialect** appeared at Kilmarnock in July 1786 in a modest edition of 612 copies at three shillings, and netted the poet about £54. Encouraged by favourable acclaim from the Revd Dr Thomas Blacklock, one of the Edinburgh literati, Burns abandoned his plans to emigrate. In

November he set out for Edinburgh in the hope of securing a second and much larger edition. Published in April 1787, this yielded about £1100, part of which Burns used to pay his brother's debts and part to take the lease of Ellisland farm in Nithsdale, which he occupied 1788-91.

At the same time, he sought a career offering a regular income and in 1789 entered the Excise service. In 1791 he abandoned farming and settled in Dumfries where he died in July 1796.

Burns's reputation as a poet rests largely on the Kilmarnock Edition of 1786 although his great comic masterpiece **Tam o' Shanter** was written in 1790. From 1787 onwards, however, Burns tended to concentrate on songs, collecting and mending the ancient ballads of Scotland, writing new verses in many cases. His importance as a folkorist and song-collector has only really been appreciated in relatively recent years, thanks to the scholarship of Professor Low and others. Many of Burns's songs were sanitised revisions of traditional bawdry, but he made a collection of the originals and composed quite a few bawdy ballads of his own; this manuscript collection was published anonymously after his death under the title of **The Merry Muses of Caledonia**, but it is only since 1968 that Burns's own contribution has been segregated and added to the canon.

The birthplace of Burns

As a poet, he was extremely versatile, handling many different metres and verse forms with consummate skill, equally at home in the verse epistle and the epigram, the sonnet and the longer satirical work. In contrast with his nature poems are the ballads savaging the hypocrisies of the Kirk and the radical songs of the 1790s. Few were published in his lifetime, but they would become the medium for extending his reputation worldwide, especially in the present century.

In addition to the 650-odd poems and songs, Burns was a voluminous letter-writer. Here again, the range of subject and treatment is wide, from the social letters to the polemics, sometimes mannered but always written with vigour, studded with colourful metaphors and containing numerous quotations and literary allusions that reveal the scope and extent of his voracious reading. Burns also had ambitions to write for the stage, but his early death left his ambition unresolved, and his only work of dramatic merit is **The Jolly Beggars, a Cantata of Love and Liberty.**

The myths of drunkenness and dissipation which grew up in the years following his death were grossly exaggerated. For the record, Burns had two sets of twins by Jean Armour before he acknowledged her formally as his wife, and five other children, the last (Maxwell Burns) being born on the day of the poet's funeral. Four other children were born out of wedlock.

In his lifetime editions of his poetry were published in Ireland and the USA and his work circulated widely in Europe, with translations into French and German from the 1820s, which had immense influence on the Romantic poets and composers. Two centuries after the Kilmarnock Edition, over 2000 editions of Burns have been published, with translations into 50 languages. Today Burns is ranked among the leading world poets of all time.

James Mackay

Lord Byron

Poet

Lord Byron

George Gordon, 6th Lord Byron, was the son of Captain John "Mad Jack" Byron (1756-91) and his second wife Catherine Gordon of Gight (d.1811) whom he married for her money (around £25,000) in 1785 and whose fortune he promptly set about ravaging. The poet was born in London on 22nd January 1788. His parents' unhappy marriage (although it is doubtful if "Mad Jack" cared whether it was "happy" or not) was sufficiently spectacular to enter the ballad record of Scotland's north east:

> *This youth is a rake, frae England is come,*
> *The Scots dinna ken his extraction ava;*
> *He keeps up his misses, his landlords he duns,*
> *That's fast drawn the lands o'Gight awa'.*

Catherine Gordon of Gight - north of Aberdeen in the valley of the Ythan - could claim descent from King James I, although the poet was to be more exercised by his Byron progenitors. His grandfather was Admiral John Byron, known as "Foulweather Jack", whose brother, the 5th Lord (1722-98) also rejoiced in a nickname - "The Wicked Lord". Had circumstances fallen out such that the poet inherited a Huntly or Gordon title then a less tormented attitude to his Scottishness could have been the result. However, it's a big "if only". Byron was a mere three-and-a-half when his prodigal father died, and six when through the death in action in Corsica of the direct heir to the Byron title, he became its heir presumptive. He attended Aberdeen Grammar School where he is remembered in G.S.Fraser's **Home Town Elegy**:

> *... Or I can make my town that homely fame*
> *That Byron has, from boys in Carden Place,*
> *Struggling home with books to midday dinner,*
> *For whom he is not the romantic sinner,*
> *The careless writer, the tormented face,*
> *The hectoring bully or the noble fool,*
> *But, just like Gordon or like Keith, a name:*
> *A tall, proud statue at the Grammar School*

While this seems reductive and Aberdonian in its way of remembering, it might be noted that Byron's romantic sinning began in Aberdeen with his first sexual experience in 1797 and his first moment of idealised love the year before. Of his cousin (distant), Mary Duff, he was to write in his journals in 1813 that he doubted if he had ever really been as sincerely attracted since. In 1798, though, with the death of "The Wicked Lord" Byron, his mother, and her maid, May Gray (she of Byron's premature sexual awakening), moved to Newstead Abbey. Within a period it became clear that hopes of enrichment or decent security were false. The Wicked Lord died skint.

Byron's status as a Scottish poet is perhaps best seen as complicated. In suggesting his Scottishness (in 1937, but collected in **On Poetry and Poets,** 1957) T.S. Eliot - who was not noted for his wisdom on Scottish matters - introduced an argument that has been simplified since. Although harried by debt and penury until his success with **Childe Harold's Pilgrimage** (1812) from late 1798 on Byron was a scion of the English aristocracy - he attended Harrow School, and Trinity College, Cambridge where he was celebrated for extravagance and outrageousness. Turbulent marriage and numerous bi-sexual amours underline the extent to which his "Mad Jack" and "Wicked Lord" antecedents were foregrounded in an extraordinary personality in which the pride of his Gordon blood and the liberal sympathies of his mother played their part. His early poem **Lachin Y Gair** is fulsome but retrospective:

> *Ah! There my young footsteps in infancy wander'd;*
> *My cap was the bonnet, my cloak was the plaid;*
> *On chieftains long perish'd my memory ponder'd,*
> *As daily I strode through the pine-cover'd glade;*

Near-Wordsworthian sentiments are filtered through the yearnings of a mind already devoted to aristocratic priorities.

The complication is enforced in Canto II of **Childe Harold's Pilgrimage** where Lord Elgin's removal of Greek statuary from the Athenian acropolis led to his denunciation as a "modern Pict". "Blush, Caledonia! such thy son could be!" is fair censure, perhaps; but "England! I joy no child he was of thine" indicates a preference even if Byron continues by regretting that the sailors who transported Elgin's plunder were Englishmen. Anti-Scottish indignation is even louder in **The Curse of Minerva** where Scotland is evoked as a "land of sophistry and mist". But the opposite point touched by the pendulum of Byron's feeling represents a massive swing. It occurs famously in Canto X of **Don Juan** where Byron addresses Lord Francis Jeffrey:

> *...for I would rather take my wine*
> *With you, than aught (save Scott) in your proud city.*

He is reacting to the phrase *Auld Lang Syne:*

> *But somehow - it may seem a schoolboy's whine,*
> *And yet I seek not to be grand nor witty,*
> *But I am half a Scot by birth, and bred*
> *A whole one, and my heart flies to my head.*

While the passage re-states Byron's Scottishness:

> *I 'scotched, not kill'd', the Scotchman in my blood,*
> *And love the land of 'mountain and of flood'.*

(with a phrase from Scott into the bargain), it does not quite reach for a reason for having neglected his Scottishness in the first place, and the implications of "scotched" are that it was deliberate, or convenient, or obligatory.

Every poet has a beginning, and Byron's earlier years were spent in Scotland, fatherless, and under the eyes of a Scottish mother and nurses. However, transformation from school in Aberdeen to an English hereditary peerage is extreme. Undoubtedly, too, it is a momentous part of what came to be responsible for a remarkable temperament - poetic, erotic, and political - that might best be considered "Byronic". Not only the geographical extent of his poetry, but his later years in Italy and Greece and affiliation with European causes suggest a degree of deracination, of profound exile, which his unique poetic intelligence may well have encouraged. His impact, too, was European. It would be difficult, perhaps impossible, to prove the Scottishness (or otherwise) of his inspiration; Byron can be claimed as a Scottish poet, but he is always likely to elude precise descriptions in such a context.

Byron died of fever at Missolonghi, Greece, on 19th April 1824 while engaged in the struggle for Greek independence.

Douglas Dunn

Thomas Campbell

Poet & journalist

Thomas Campbell

Thomas Campbell was born in Glasgow on 27th July 1777. He was the eleventh child of a family descended from the Campbells of Kirnan in Argyllshire. His father, a wealthy tobacco trader, was financially ruined when the American colonies seceded. At school and university Campbell won prizes for verse translations from the Classics and for a poetical essay, **On the Origin of Evil**. Time spent as a tutor in Mull and Lochgilphead gave a feeling for the Highlands expressed later in poems like **Lord Ullin's Daughter**, **Lochiel's Warning** and **Glenara**. Unsure of his future he went to Edinburgh to study law, but attracted by a literary career he achieved remarkable success with the publication in 1799 of a long poem in heroic couplets, **The Pleasures of Hope**. In this poem, a survey of human affairs, he wrote of the sufferings caused by partition to the people of Poland. He campaigned obsessively for the Polish cause. In 1800 he visited Germany and saw the evidence of war including an Austrian cavalry charge at Ratisbon, the site of the battle fought at Hohenlinden in December 1800, and, when sailing home, the Danish batteries and the British fleet which took part in the battle of Copenhagen. These sights inspired his martial poems, **Ye Mariners of England**, **Hohenlinden** and **The Battle of the Baltic**. His patriotic verse won him early recognition in 1805 with the grant of a government pension. With great industry but less permanent success he wrote long narrative poems, including **Gertrude of Wyoming**, a sad tale of settlers and Red Indians in Pennsylvania. It is noteworthy as the first long poem with an American setting by a British author.

Campbell was a versatile, professional writer and not solely a poet. He wrote for newspapers, compiled biographies, contributed articles to encyclopaedias, and from 1820 to 1831 edited, **The New Monthly Review**. His **Specimens of the British Poets**, extended to seven volumes of selected passages from writers, with biography and criticism.

In 1825 he wrote to Lord Brougham to initiate a scheme to establish a university in London. He took great pride in the ultimate success of his proposal with the establishment of an institution that became University College. His wide-spread popularity was confirmed when Glasgow University students elected him their Rector in 1827, 1828 and 1829.

Campbell was part of a literary tradition which was both highly academic and English. A skilful metrist, he engaged in constant revision of his work, very possibly to its detriment. His early, shorter poems had more enduring appeal and eleven of them appear in **Palgrave's Golden Treasury**, many more than all except the greatest lyric poets. He wrote many quotable lines, some now commonplace expressions, as "Tis distance lends enchantment to the view", "And coming events cast their shadows before." Few now read his work. But how many read Milton's?

Campbell's wife and two sons pre-deceased him. He died in Boulogne on 15th June, 1844 and is buried in Westminster Abbey.

J. Cuthbert Hadden, **Thomas Campbell**, Oliphant, Anderson and Ferrier, 1900.
Poems (Complete Edition), ed. J. Logie Robertson, Cambridge University Press, 1907.

John Gilfillan

Thomas Carlyle

Historian, essayist & critic

Thomas Carlyle

Thomas Carlyle was born in Ecclefechan on 5th December 1795, son of a hard-working and pious stonemason. Father and mother both destined their eldest son for the Church, and were to be lifelong influences: they instilled a strong sense of belief, of divine order, of the importance of hard work. They also helped by example to sharpen a formidable style, both spoken and written.

Edinburgh University followed local schools; rapidly losing any ambition for the Church Carlyle tried school teaching, translation, scientific writing, tutoring, the law — slowly working his way to modest success as essayist, translator, biographer, and by the late 1820s to public notice as author of important essays **Signs of the Times, Characteristics** and an astonishing early work, **Sartor Resartus** in which Carlyle anticipates many features of twentieth century writing, stripping off the rotting fabric of belief in his own age, and calling for a radical re-think and renewal.

Carlyle was among the first critics to see the dangers of relying too much on the mechanical marvels of his age.

> *Not the external and physical alone is now managed by machinery, but the internal and spiritual also. Here too nothing follows its spontaneous course, nothing is left to be accomplished by the old natural methods … Men are grown mechanical in head and in heart, as well as in hand.*

Carlyle devoted his writing career to countering that mechanising tendency in society and in individuals. He produced outstanding histories (notably of the French Revolution, but also of Cromwell and Frederick the Great) and works which pungently attack the spiritual deadness of the times — **Latter-Day Pamphlets, Past and Present.** Perhaps his most effective writing is in **Heroes and Hero-Worship**, a call for renewal in the nineteenth century on heroic principles, the identification of heroes to lead a society which had lost its way.

As he grew older Carlyle moved to the Right, losing his earlier radicalism in an insistence on order in a society which often seemed to veer towards revolution. Carlyle, after all, had grown up in the bloody aftermath of the French Revolution. His readers split between those who supported him, and those who felt he had lost touch with the needs of his age. But his core reputation remained, and remains. His effect on contemporary writers was extraordinary, and above all the Victorian novel bears the imprint of his analysis of the times — Dickens, Thackeray, Eliot, Disraeli all could not have written as they did without his example.

He died in 1881, and after decades of eclipse his reputation is steadily rising. Not only is he a formative Victorian, a great Scottish writer who outlived most of his contemporaries; he and his gifted wife Jane Welsh (1801-66) are being revealed, in their collected correspondence, as among the greatest letter-writers ever. Together, they knew a cross section of Victorian Britain which makes their writings and letters a priceless introduction to an age of change and enormous energy.

Ian Campbell

Catherine Carswell
Novelist & biographer

Catherine Carswell

Carswell was born Catherine Roxburgh Macfarlane in Glasgow on 27th March 1879. She was educated there, reading English at Glasgow University, and spent two years studying music in Frankfurt. She married in 1904, but the marriage was annulled on the grounds of her husband's severe mental illness, and she embarked on a long relationship with the painter Maurice Greiffenhagen. Already a reviewer for the **Glasgow Herald**, she moved to London in 1912, and in 1915 married a fellow journalist, Donald Carswell.

Meanwhile she had become friendly with D. H. Lawrence, and lost her post on the **Glasgow Herald** when she reviewed his novel **The Rainbow** against the editor's wishes. Lawrence encouraged her in the writing of her first novel **Open the Door!** (1920). His influence, along with a strong autobiographical element, can be seen in the novel, but **Open the Door!** is particularly notable for its frank treatment, unusual in women's writing of the time, of developing independence and sexuality in its heroine Joanna Bannerman:

> *Wave after wave of purely physical recollections swept through her; but at the same time in her brain a cool spectator seemed to be sitting aloof and in judgment. This then was marriage! This droll device, this astonishing grotesque experience was what the poets had sung since the beginning. To this all her quivering dreams had led, all Mario's wooing touches and his glances of fire!*

The central character of her second novel, **The Camomile** (1922), has, like Carswell herself, studied music, but now feels herself drawn to writing. In her milieu of turn-of-the-century Glasgow this is not seen as a "womanly" occupation, and the novel is a serious examination, though in readable epistolary form, of the particular problems and dilemmas faced by a woman writer.

The Carswells were now both attempting to live by freelance writing, and Catherine's work - reviewing, criticism and editing - provided a major part of the family income. She wrote no more novels, but, in what time could be spared from journalism, produced her groundbreaking **Life of Robert Burns** (1930). Returning to original sources and avoiding the near-idolatrous view of Burns then current, the biography met with much criticism from Burnsians, but is now well regarded for its perception and style, and has recently been reissued. Two other biographies followed: **The Savage Pilgrimage** (1932), a memoir of D. H. Lawrence (which also ran into trouble on publication, encountering objections from another Lawrence biographer), and **The Tranquil Heart** (1937), a biography of the fourteenth-century Italian writer Boccaccio, whom she also admired.

Catherine Carswell died on 19th March 1946. Her fragmentary papers and autobiographical writings were edited by her son and published as **Lying Awake: an unfinished autobiography** (1950). Forgotten or undervalued for some thirty years, her work was rediscovered in the 1980s, when Virago reissued **Open the Door!** and **The Camomile**, and she is now recognised as an important figure in Scottish women's writing. A first volume of criticism, **Essays on Catherine Carswell**, edited by Carol Anderson, is forthcoming from Ramsay Head Press.

Moira Burgess

Joe Corrie

Playwright, poet, journalist & short story writer

Joe Corrie

Joe Corrie was born in Slamannan in 1894 and, after his family's move to Cardenden in Fife, he left school in 1908 to work in the local pit. As a result of his father's ill-health and consequent family poverty Corrie's formal education was patchy but as a young man he attended classes run by the Workers' Educational Association and had access to the library of the Miners' Welfare Institute.

It was during the 1920s that Corrie began writing and his plays, poems, journalism and short stories reflect the harsh living and working conditions of the Fife mining community. A fortnightly column in **The Miner** led to the publication of articles in other socialist newspapers. The first volume of Corrie's poems, **The Image o' God and Other Poems**, protesting against the social consequences of poverty and deprivation was published in 1928 and **Rebel Poems** was published by the Independent Labour Party in 1932.

First performances of Corrie's one-act plays **Hogmanay** and **The Shillin'-a-week Man** were given in 1926 by the amateur Bowhill Players to raise funds for miners' soup kitchens. Corrie's first full-length play, **In Time o' Strife** (1927), was written after the General Strike and depicts its divisive effects on the Fife mining community. It was rejected by the Scottish National Players, which led to an acrimonious debate in the Scottish press during 1929. The play was toured, to great acclaim, throughout Central Scotland by the Bowhill Players who, for a short time, became a professional theatre company - the Fife Miner Players. Contemporary critics began to speak of Corrie as the "Scottish Zola" or Scotland's answer to Sean O'Casey but the theatrical establishment continued to demonstrate a strong antipathy to the socialist bias in his dramatisation of Scottish working class life. Corrie's political stance is illustrated in the final lines of **In Time o' Strife**. Jenny, one of the strong matriarchal figures featured in many Corrie plays, speaks while voices singing **The Red Flag** are heard in the distance:

> *(... SHE SPEAKS, AS IF INSPIRED BY SOME GREAT HOPE.)*
>
> *That's the spirit, my he'rties! sing! sing! tho' they ha'e ye chained to the wheels and the darkness. Sing! tho' they ha'e ye crushed in the mire. Keep up your he'rts, my laddies, you'll win through yet, for there's nae power on earth can crush the men that can sing on a day like this.*

Rejected by the professional theatre Corrie continued to earn a living by writing more than fifty one-act plays for performance by the hundreds of amateur theatre groups who were members of the Scottish Community Drama Association. Although enormously popular, many of these plays are light-weight comedies and romances. During the 1930s, as a result of his relationship with some of the more radical groups, Corrie wrote some of his best short plays, including **Hewers of Coal** (1936/7). Joe Corrie is quoted as saying that he liked to give his audiences a good cry and a good laugh. He died in Edinburgh on 13th November 1968.

Chris Ravenhall

S R Crockett

Novelist

S R Crockett

Born in Balmaghie, Kirkcudbrightshire, in 1859, Samuel Rutherford Crockett was the illegitimate son of a dairymaid whose parents, although Cameronians, were too proud to have her marry for mere respectability. Of tenant farming stock, they brought him up in a happy country childhood; from the Free Church school at Castle Douglas he won a bursary to Edinburgh University. Thereafter he travelled on the Continent as a tutor, then entered New College, Edinburgh, as a student for the Free Church ministry. He became Free Church minister at Penicuik, Midlothian, in 1886. He married the daughter of a philanthropic Manchester mill-owner and had four children.

He continued his journalism during his ministry. Lively sketches of Scottish ministers and congregations were so popular in their slightly sardonic humour that some twenty-four of them published in 1893 as **The Stickit Minister** brought fame. The success in 1894 of **The Raiders** and **The Lilac Sunbonnet**, both set in Galloway, the one adventure, the other a romance, led him to embark on full-time writing; he had in any case grown increasingly impatient with the narrow outlook of the Free Church.

Often maligned as "Kailyard", Crockett could from experience write of the slums of Edinburgh, of coalminers and factory workers and of the countries he had visited; even when treating country themes he did not always present idyllic pictures. He wrote vigorously and sometimes sensationally of Galloway Covenanters in **Men of the Moss Hags**; of feuding seventeenth-century Kennedies in **The Grey Man,** including Sawney Bean the legendary cannibal; of Edinburgh waifs and railwaymen in **Cleg Kelly**; of the noble fifteenth-century Douglases in **Black Douglas** and **Maid Margaret** - with a touch of sorcery; of French Huguenots in **The White Plumes of Navarre**. His range was wide but uneven. He did not maintain his first popularity, perhaps because of this very versatility — every Crockett was different from the one before.

His health deteriorated, but his agent urged him to keep his illnesses secret. He had to spend winters abroad, in Spain or France, and return home only for the summers. But he remained always cheerful and hopeful, using all his interests to write not works of genius but lively narratives with a sardonic flavour.

The burns were running red with the mighty July rain when Douglas Maclellan started over the meadows and moors to preach his sermon at the farmtown of Cauldshaws. He had thanked the Lord that morning in his opening prayer for "the bounteous rain wherewith He had seen meet to refresh his weary heritage,"

His congregation silently acquiesced, "for what," said they, "could a man from the Machars be expected to ken about meadow hay?"

He died very suddenly in Tarascon in France in April 1914. His body was brought back to Balmaghie for burial, to lie "among the dear and simple folk I knew and loved in youth", as he had always hoped.

Francis Russell Hart, **The Scottish Novel. A Critical Survey**, Murray, 1978.
Islay M. Donaldson, **Samuel Rutherford Crockett**, AUP, 1989.

Islay M. Donaldson

A J Cronin

A J Cronin

Novelist

Archibald Joseph Cronin, the creator of Doctor Finlay, was born on 19th July 1896 in Cardross near Dumbarton, in the midst of the area which was to provide a source and inspiration for a number of his novels, more particularly **Hatter's Castle,** the best selling first novel which catapulted him to worldwide fame in 1930. As the son of a mixed marriage of Protestant mother and Catholic father, he was brought up as a Catholic, but attended Dumbarton Academy because of his precocious abilities. Years later he wrote:

> *A feeling of social inferiority was immediately … communicated to me, a sort of spiritual wound deriving from my religion,*

so it is possible that a feeling of alienation from the West of Scotland may have contributed to his long exile.

At Glasgow University he studied medicine with some distinction and after war service as a Royal Navy surgeon - one of several echoes of another Dumbartonshire novelist, Tobias Smollett - Cronin entered general practice and went to work in a mining area of South Wales. Again this experience and his subsequent move to a fashionable practice in Harley Street was to provide inspiration - most obviously for **The Citadel**, which was at the same time his most commercially successful and his most crusading work. It has been said that its exposure of inequalities in medical provision contributed to the introduction of the National Health Service.

Cronin tends to be classed nowadays as being among the first of the formula writers, very dependent on the shrewd marketing skills of his publisher, Gollancz. Certainly, his success was staggering by any yardstick. **The Citadel,** for example, broke all publishing records and sold at the rate of 10,000 hardback copies a week for months on end. A "blockbuster" then, but not without critical approval. Hugh Walpole called **Hatter's Castle** the finest first novel since the Great War, while others were quick to spot a vivid cinematic quality in the novels - indeed many were made into successful films. Here is a scene from **Hatter's Castle,** in which Brodie the bullying patriarch is cross-examining his daughter Mary about a young man:

> *An unconscious force drove her to say in a low, firm voice:*
> *"He's not a worthless scamp."*
> *"What!" roared Brodie. "You're speaking back to your own father next and for a low down Irish blackguard! A blackthorn boy! No! Let these paddies come over from their bogs to dig our potatoes for us but let it end at that. Don't let them get uppish".*

By the 1970s, however, Cronin's reputation was slight and later novels like **A Song of Sixpence** attracted fewer readers, although the new medium of television indirectly claimed new fans, through the Doctor Finlay stories. He withdrew to what was assumed to be a tax exile in Switzerland and died there in 1981, generally supposed to be a millionaire, in that respect a rarity among Scottish writers. **The Times** obituary judged that his had been "'middlebrow' fiction of the most adroit and telling kind."

Ronald Armstrong

Helen Cruickshank

Poet, cultural & political activist

Photo: Gordon Wright

Helen Cruickshank

Helen Burness Cruickshank was born on 15th May 1886, in Hillside, near Montrose, of local parents, and went to school in Montrose. Summer holidays were spent in Glenesk and the landscapes and people of Angus and its glens appear in her poetry. After leaving school, Cruickshank entered the Civil Service, working first in London, and then, from 1912, in Edinburgh, where she spent most of her adult life. She joined the Women's Social and Political Union, and actively campaigned for the Suffragette cause. She was also a committed Scottish nationalist, an active member of the Saltire Society, and a founder member of Scottish PEN, which she served in various ways. She encouraged the work of the young C.M. Grieve (Hugh MacDiarmid), of James Leslie Mitchell (Lewis Grassic Gibbon), and other writers, and was sympathetic in her appreciation of the poetry of Violet Jacob and Marion Angus. Helen Cruickshank devoted much of her life to other people (she cared for her elderly mother), yet published poetry over several decades, in **Scottish Chapbook, Northern Numbers** and many other journals, and in **Up the Noran Water** (1934), **Sea Buckthorn** (1954), **The Ponnage Pool** (1968), **Collected Poems** (1971) and **More Collected Poems** (1978).

Helen Cruickshank's best known poem is probably **Shy Geordie**, which, like much of her work, is in Scots and draws on her Angus country heritage (the poem has been set to music by several people, including Buxton Orr and Jim Reid). Many of her poems echo ballad and folk-song and other traditional forms. **In Glenskenno Woods, There was a Sang** or **Fause Friend** may appear simple, but they show a range of mood and tone, from lyrical to humorous, and her best work avoids the charge of sentimentality which might sometimes be levelled. She draws on the natural world for strong symbols about human life, as in the fine **Sea Buckthorn** (set to music by Francis George Scott), or in **The Ponnage Pool**, prefaced with a quotation from Hugh MacDiarmid; this deals with questions of personal identity:

> I mind o' the Ponnage Pule,
> The reid brae risin',
> Morphie Lade,
> An' the saumon that louped the dam,
> A tree i' Martin's Den
> Wi' names carved on it;
> But I ken na wha I am.

Cruickshank also wrote in English; her poem **Spring in the Mearns** for instance, is a tribute to Lewis Grassic Gibbon. **Lines for Wendy Wood** celebrate another activist; this poem also illustrates Cruickshank's own passionate concern with social problems, her compassion and commitment to the fighting of poverty and injustice, shown, too, in a Scots poem such as **Song of Pity for Refugees**.

Although Cruickshank recorded her long life and aspects of her times in her **Octobiography** (1978), the significance of her generous contribution to the cultural life of Scotland still awaits a full estimation. Helen Cruickshank died in 1975.

Carol Anderson

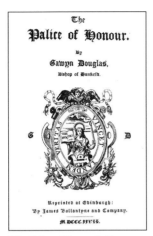

The
Palice of Honour.
By
Gawyn Douglas,
Bishop of Dunkeld.

Reprinted at Edinburgh:
By James Ballantyne and Company.
M.DCCC.XXVII.

"The Palice of Honour" title page.

Gavin Douglas

Poet

Gavin Douglas (c.1476-1522) was a younger son of Archibald Douglas, fifth Earl of Angus; membership of this powerful family clearly aided his early rise to high office in the church. Douglas was educated at the University of St Andrews, graduating in 1494. He possibly later studied in Paris. By 1503 he held several minor benefices, and was provost of the important collegiate church of St Giles, Edinburgh. He was a highly ambitious man, and during the troubled minority of James V sought further promotion in the church, becoming Bishop of Dunkeld in 1516. Later in the reign Douglas's association with the cause of his nephew Archibald, sixth Earl of Angus (whom he privately called a "witless fuill"), brought him into conflict with the regent, the Duke of Albany; he fled to England and died in exile in London in 1522.

All Douglas's surviving works belong to the early part of his life during the reign of James IV. **The Palice of Honour** is a complex allegorical dream-poem, dedicated to the King and probably composed in 1501. The nature of honour was a topic much discussed in the sixteenth century; Douglas here attributes highest value to heroic honour, won by virtue and courage in battle, but he implies that for himself the most congenial route to honour is poetry. The work is highly introspective, and enlivened by dry wit and irony.

Douglas's most famous poem is a translation of Virgil's **Aeneid**, completed in 1513 just before the battle of Flodden. **The Eneados**, to use Douglas's own title, was a pioneering work; the first of the great Renaissance translations from the classics, and one closely based (which was not then a common practice) on Virgil's own text. Douglas was fired by a double purpose: to transfer to his native tongue something of the "fouth", or linguistic richness, of Latin, and also to communicate an intimate knowledge of Virgil's great poem to his countrymen.

The translation is in heroic couplets, and a little more diffuse than Virgil. Where Douglas is most successful is in descriptive passages - the hunt in book IV, battle-scenes, and storms at sea - or portraits, such as those of Charon, the ferryman of hell, and Venus disguised as a huntress,

> With wynd waving hir haris lowsit [loosened] of tres,
> Hir skirt kiltit til hir bair kne (I. vi. 26-7).

Much of Douglas's most original writing is found in the Prologues that he provided for each book. These illuminate his principles and methods as a translator; and three, depicting a frosty December, a May morning, and a June night, reveal his genius for precise and sensuous description of the natural world. The Prologues convey a vivid sense of Douglas's personality, lively, bookish, and argumentative.

The link with Virgil is what kept Douglas's name alive, during the centuries when many early Scottish poets were forgotten. Today, however, he is highly appreciated, both as an excellent translator and also as a poet with a distinctive voice and remarkable "fouth" of language.

Virgil's Aeneid Translated into Scottish Verse by Gavin Douglas, ed. David F. C. Coldwell, 4 vols. Scottish Text Society, Edinburgh, 1957-64.
Priscilla Bawcutt, **Gavin Douglas: a Critical Study**, Edinburgh, 1976.

Priscilla Bawcutt

Arthur Ignatius Conan Doyle

Short story writer, novelist, journalist & doctor

Conan Doyle was born in Edinburgh, 22nd May 1859, to Roman Catholic parents of Irish origin. Educated locally and by the Jesuits at Stonyhurst College, the boy then graduated from Edinburgh University in medicine in 1881. His first short story had been published in **Chambers's Journal** in September 1879, and his first non-fiction in the **British Medical Journal** the same month.

A crude, unpublished story from this time shows him experimenting with two lead characters, a daring master of arcane scientific perceptions and a down-to-earth narrator inviting audience identification, but it was not until 1886 that the ultimate development of the two types came to life in **A Study in Scarlet** as the consulting detective Sherlock Holmes and his fellow-lodger Dr Watson. Their brilliant, ironic, infectious dialogue, to be continued over fifty six short stories and four novels in all, originally derived from Plato's Socrates and his disciples, Cervantes's Don Quixote and Sancho Panza, and James Boswell's conversations with Dr Samuel Johnson, but many of the initial strokes of characterization derived from Conan Doyle's medical teachers, fellow-students, and former Jesuit masters.

Sherlock Holmes

Conan Doyle also acknowledged his debt to Edgar Allan Poe, father of the detective-story, but for all of his readiness to belittle his own creation by comparison, Sherlock Holmes became inescapably identified as the heroic Great Detective, all the more when Conan Doyle, fearing Holmes would eclipse his historical fiction, tried to kill him off in 1893. The interval between the high drama of **The Final Problem** where Holmes apparently sacrifices his life to eliminate the "Napoleon of Crime" Professor Moriarty, and **The Hound of the Baskervilles**, his reappearance eight years later, gave his creator space to produce the finest series of historical short stories ever written, the exploits of the Napoleonic soldier, Etienne Gerard, miniature revitalisations of the past admirably counterpointing Tolstoy's **War and Peace.**

Conan Doyle's long stories included medieval narratives of the fourteenth-century nomadic soldiery, of the Monmouth Rebellion and the Huguenots, of Regency England and of Arab revolt in the Sudan. But the short story was his classical art-form, and the precision, clarity, wit, pace, atmosphere, intellectual debate were achieved initially through training in case-study narrative from his medical education. Very appropriately, his later work included science-fiction adventures once again utilising learned but hilarious Edinburgh academics as models, the Professor Challenger stories.

The popularity of so much of Conan Doyle's work stood in the way of its academic recognition but the Holmes tales have now received critical editions and the Gerard has won scholarly presentation. Conan Doyle himself practised in Portsmouth as a doctor from 1882, but abandoned medicine for literature in 1891, moving to London, and later to Sussex and Essex. He became a Spiritualist after World War I (of which he had written histories), a religious interest which enhanced his tales of the macabre. He died in 1930 having been married twice and fathered five children.

Owen Dudley Edwards

William Drummond of Hawthornden

Poet

William Drummond

William Drummond was born at Hawthornden, Midlothian, in 1585, and died there in 1649. Drummond's father, Sir John, was gentleman-usher to James VI and accompanied the King to England in 1603. His mother, Susannah, was sister to the Scottish court poet, William Fowler. Traditionally, Drummond would have been regarded as a hereditary poet.

Graduating MA in 1605 at Edinburgh University, Drummond travelled to the Continent to study law. His father's death in 1610 made him laird of Hawthornden. He returned to the seclusion of his estate by the Esk, and read widely in European languages, especially Italian. He collected the works of contemporary Scots and English poets too, amassing his famous library of over 550 books which he gifted to Edinburgh University.

Rarely leaving Hawthornden, he divided his time between his poetry and his mechanical inventions. His chief poetical works are: **Teares on the Death of Meliades** (1613) a lament on the death of Prince Henry; **Poems** (1616), **Forth Feasting** (1617) for the King's visit to Edinburgh; **Flowres of Sion** (1623), Scotland's finest collection of divine poems in that century; **To the Exequies of Sir Antonye Alexander** (1638), a pastoral elegy. He is also credited with the comic verses **Polemo-Medinia**, or "the midden-fecht'', in Scots mixed with dog Latin.

The finest Scottish poet of his day, he is at his best in his sonnets, particularly in his mastery of the final couplet. He prizes a flowing smoothness, full of natural grace and passionate feeling, very Italianate, and he loves to decorate his verse in the mannerist style. He keeps many of the features of the older Scots poetry, especially his skill in metrics and in melody. Drummond's poems express his love of creation by a dynamic control of syntax linked to metrical fluency.

Drummond was admired by his contemporaries. Through his poetry he won the friendship of poets such as Alexander, Drayton and Jonson. **Notes of Ben Jonson's Conversations at Hawthornden** give evidence of a congenial friendship and a stimulating freedom of speech.

He tried to avoid political involvement, but in troubled times he had to appear before covenanting committees and defend his writings, which he did on the basis of liberty of opinion. He refused an instruction "to ravage and plunder the more peaceable neighbours about". He sympathised with Montrose, and in 1645 Montrose, at the head of the royalist army, issued orders that Drummond, and Hawthornden, were specially protected. Drummond wrote his essay, **Irene**, as a plea for peace.

Men thirled to the fortunes of the court or of the battlefield, like Kerr or Montrose, looked to Drummond as their ideal personified, the "happy man" in the classical sense, who led a life which they hoped to emulate some day.

Drummond can be regarded as the first Scots poet to write in English, the forerunner of a tradition extending to today's Morgan or MacCaig. His poetry claims descent from the old Scots court poetry, but it looks to Europe and his literary boundaries overshoot those of nationality. He is part of European literature, his style developing the work of Bembo, Marino and Tasso.

Valerie Gillies

William Dunbar

Poet

Dunbar (c.1460-c.1513) has left vivid images of Scotland in the reign of James IV, yet much in his own life, including the dates of his birth and death, remains obscure. **The Flyting**, a verse quarrel between Dunbar and another poet, Walter Kennedy, offers information as to his ancestry, character and personal appearance, but in this type of poem it is difficult to determine how much truth lies beneath the scurrilous insults. Dunbar, however, was certainly a Lowlander, from the Lothian region, and spent many years in Edinburgh. He was well educated, and took a bachelor's degree at the University of St Andrews in 1477 and a master's degree in 1479. Nothing definite is known of his activities between 1480 and 1500, although he may have been abroad: some of his poems imply familiarity with Denmark and France, and in the winter of 1500-1501 he was apparently in England.

The best-documented period of Dunbar's life is from 1500 to 1513; during this time he received a "pensioun", or annual salary from James IV, as a member of the royal household. By 1504 he had taken priest's orders, and is later referred to as a "chaplain"; several poems voice his hopes for a benefice, yet he is not known ever to have obtained even a humble parish kirk. Well-educated churchmen at this time carried out many of the tasks of government, and it is likely that Dunbar had some role in the royal secretariat, as a clerk or envoy. His poems reveal familiarity with legal usage and terminology, and he occasionally acted as a procurator, or advocate, in the law courts. The last mention of Dunbar in the court records is on 14th May 1513, but there is a gap in these records following the battle of Flodden (September 1513), in which the King died; Dunbar may have survived into the reign of James V, but there is no positive evidence that he did so.

The Scottish court provided Dunbar with his livelihood and also with his primary audience. Many of his poems are addressed to the king or queen, or refer to fellow-courtiers, ranging from humble fools to powerful officials, such as the Treasurer. The **Thrissill and the Rose** celebrates the wedding of James IV to Margaret Tudor in 1503, and other poems are concerned with festive events in this reign, such as the Tournament of the Black Lady (1507), the arrival of the French envoy Bernard Stewart in 1508, and the Queen's visit to Aberdeen in 1511. But many of Dunbar's poems cast a more satiric eye at the activities of James IV's court, and convey an uneasy atmosphere of self-seeking, envy and distrust.

Dunbar's favourite term for his own writings was *ballatis*, a word that then usually connoted short, often lyrical poems. Dunbar indeed stands out from other late medieval poets for the brevity and compression of his verse. He also called himself a *makar*, a term that lays stress on the poet as a skilled and versatile craftsman. Dunbar is famed for his virtuosity, and was ready to write on almost any subject, from a painful headache to a highly technical treatise on penance. He experimented with many popular genres - elegy, panegyric, love epistle, beast fable, satiric testament - but shows particular fondness for the medieval tradition of dream poetry. His dream poems are characteristically varied: the most famous is **The Goldyn Targe**, a complex courtly allegory, in which love triumphs over reason; another is a

Chepman's imprint of a Dunbar ballade

devout vision of the Crucifixion, whose tone recalls the Mystery plays; and several others, grotesque in style and satirical in purpose, might better be described as nightmares. Dunbar is also an accomplished metrist. **The Twa Mariit Wemen and the Wedo** shows his mastery of alliterative verse, but he also employs a variety of stanzas, ranging from rhyme royal to the popular carol. Many of his poems make a witty use of refrains.

The degree of self-expression in Dunbar has been much debated. His few love poems are highly conventional, and the "I" of several didactic pieces seems largely a mouthpiece for orthodox morality. But poems such as **In to thir dirk and drublie dayis** and **I that in heill wes** (often called **The Lament for the Makaris**) communicate, simply yet very poignantly, Dunbar's personal response to death:

> *Sen he [Death] has all my brether tane*
> *He will naught lat me lif alane;*
> *On forse I man [must] hys nyxt pray be:*
> *Timor mortis conturbat me.*

Although Dunbar is not a profoundly autobiographical poet, his most intimate-sounding voice is heard in the petitions, a small group of verse epistles, addressed chiefly to the King. Their tone is characteristically half-humorous, and half-melancholy; in one of the most successful Dunbar adopts the persona of an old horse to convey his sense of rejection by the King.

Many of Dunbar's most original poems are sardonic and mocking in tone. His targets include the familiar butts of late medieval comedy, such as friars or tailors, but also extend to himself, his friends, and fellow-courtiers. Perhaps the blackest comedy is to be found in **The Twa Mariit Wemen and the Wedo**, in which three young women talk uninhibitedly of love, men and marriage. Much influenced by the traditions of anti-feminist satire, this is Dunbar's longest and most ambitious work. Dunbar also had a talent for parody and burlesque, best illustrated by **The Testament of Master Andro Kennedy**, and **The Dirige**, a small comic masterpiece.

Dunbar is a master stylist. Bold and self-confident in his use of language, he is highly sensitive both to the sound and the connotations of words. He ranges from the high, often Latinate style of **The Goldyn Targe** to the low, colloquial, vulgar diction of **The Flyting**. He seizes the reader's attention by arresting first lines, such as the explosive opening to his fine poem on the Resurrection: "Done is a battell on the dragon blak". Dunbar's verse abounds in unusual imagery, and is rich in irony, puns, and other forms of word-play.

Dunbar is not a learned or intellectual writer, but he is the most brilliant of the early Scottish poets. Despite the lapse of five centuries he retains a power to move, to entertain, and even to shock his readers. It is not surprising that when Hugh MacDiarmid sought a new model for modern Scottish poetry - tough, witty, and unsentimental - he adopted as his slogan, "Not Burns - Dunbar!"

The Poems of William Dunbar, ed. James Kinsley, Oxford, 1979.
William Dunbar: Selected Poems, ed. Priscilla Bawcutt, London, 1996.
Ian S. Ross, **William Dunbar**, Leiden, 1981.
Priscilla Bawcutt, **Dunbar the Makar**, Oxford, 1992.

Priscilla Bawcutt

Jane Duncan
Novelist

Jane Duncan

"Jane Duncan" was the pseudonym used by Elizabeth Jane Cameron, who was born in Renton, Dumbartonshire, on 10th March 1910. Childhood holidays were spent in the Black Isle, Easter Ross, on her grandparents' croft "The Colony", which is the "Reachfar" of her novels. She graduated from Glasgow University and served in the WAAF during World War II. She lived in Jamaica for ten years, returning to Scotland in 1958 on the death of her husband.

Though she had enjoyed writing all her life, Duncan did not seek publication until her husband's serious illness. Still in Jamaica, in need of money and facing the prospect of widowhood, she submitted a novel to an agent in London, and, when it was accepted, revealed that she had completed six further manuscripts. They became the first volumes in the **My Friends** series, which eventually comprised 19 titles. **My Friends the Miss Boyds** (1959), an immediate success on publication, begins the story of Janet Sandison, the narrator and central character of the series. Janet's life in the novels corresponds closely to the author's own, and Duncan's autobiographical work **Letter from Reachfar** (1975) identifies the source of many of her fictional characters and events.

Duncan's aim was to delineate Janet's character as it might be revealed gradually in conversation with a friend. Originally the reader was to meet her as an adult in **My Friend Muriel**, learning about her happy childhood (**The Miss Boyds**) and troubled adolescence (**Annie**) much later in the series. The publishers' decision to begin with **The Miss Boyds** and continue in chronological sequence negated this more subtle and considered approach Beyond this, Duncan is exploring the reality of "Reachfar", which Janet cherishes throughout her life as a symbol of innocence and truth:

> *Those days had come forward through life with me, a permanent background, clearly outlined in the brilliant northern light, that had influenced - and for good, I thought — every new experience that slid on to the stage of life in front of it. The light from that background had, for me, illumined everything.*

But the idyllic "Reachfar" of **The Miss Boyds** is physically all but destroyed by the time of **My Friends George and Tom** (1976), and Janet has sensed its spiritual vulnerability long before. Duncan's novels, readable and popular, are often dismissed as light fiction, but Francis Russell Hart considers them at some length in **The Scottish Novel** (1978).

Duncan also published four novels under the pseudonym "Janet Sandison", beginning with **Jean in the Morning** (1969). These were supposed, on one level at least, to be the novels which Janet, in the **My Friends** series, is writing in secret. Set in a Lowland town, they are generally considered less successful than the Reachfar books.

Duncan's later novels, with the children's stories which she wrote for, and fictionally about, her niece and nephews, were written at Jemimaville in Easter Ross, in the area of the original "Reachfar", where she lived from 1958 onwards. She died there on 20th October 1976.

Moira Burgess

Robert Fergusson

Poet

Robert Fergusson

Robert Fergusson was born in Edinburgh on 5th September 1750, of Aberdeenshire parents. He attended the High School in Edinburgh before obtaining a bursary to Dundee Grammar School in 1762. The bursary also took him on to the University of St Andrews in 1765, but his father's death in May 1767 led him to leave the university the following year without taking his degree: he had to return to Edinburgh to support his mother and younger sister, and obtained the humble position of clerk or copyist to the Commissary Office at the rate of a penny per page transcribed.

At St Andrews Fergusson led a lively social life. He sang, he engaged in student pranks, and in April 1765 he wrote his first known poem, **Elegy on the Death of Mr David Gregory, late Professor of Mathematics in the University of St Andrews**. This poem — lively, humorous, half a mock-elegy and half serious — is in an old Scottish tradition of mock-elegy in Scots and shows Fergusson's interest in the Scots language and in Scots poetic forms at a time when most educated Scotsmen used English models in their writing. The skill, vigour, wit and sheer confidence shown in this poem indicated a talent already well developed and the use of Scots is assured and adroit.

For the rest of his short life, passed in Edinburgh, Fergusson regularly contributed poems to **The Weekly Magazine or Edinburgh Amusement** published by Thomas Ruddiman. He led a lively social life, frequently attending the theatre and making friends with actors. He was a member of the Cape Club, a society whose membership included painters, musicians and actors and covered a wide range of social classes. The Club met in various Edinburgh taverns to celebrate poetry and song.

Fergusson's first contributions to **The Weekly Magazine** were based on English models, but he soon showed his true genius for poetry in Scots with **The Daft Days**, a splendidly vivid celebratory poem in an old Scottish tradition. In the Scots poems that followed he showed his developing skills in descriptive, celebratory, patriotic and satirical poetry with a flexible use of the Scots language and a remarkable combination of vernacular vigour and classical assurance. These poems included **Elegy on the Death of Scots Music, The King's Birth-Day in Edinburgh, Caller Oysters, Hallow Fair, The Rising of the Session, The Sitting of the Session, Caller Water, The Ghaists; A Kirk-yard Eclogue, Leith Races, The Farmer's Ingle** (on which Burns modelled his **Cotter's Saturday Night**), and the remarkable long poem on Edinburgh, **Auld Reekie**.

Fergusson's language shows a range and assurance not seen in Scots since the Makars. In his tragically short poetic career (he died in 1774) he re-established Scots poetry and made Burns possible.

Poems of Robert Fergusson, edited by M. P. McDiarmid. Scottish Text Society, 2 vols. Edinburgh and London, 1947-56

S. G. Smith (ed.) **Robert Fergusson, Essays by various hands**, Edinburgh, 1942.

D. Daiches, **Robert Fergusson**, Edinburgh, 1982.

David Daiches

Susan Edmonstone Ferrier

Novelist

Susan Ferrier was born in Edinburgh on 17th September 1782, daughter of Helen Coutts and James Ferrier, a Writer to the Signet. As a child, Ferrier accompanied her father to Inveraray Castle, Loch Fyne whenever his business as manager of the estates of the fifth Duke of Argyll took him north. These trips across the Highland line gave Ferrier the setting for her novels and two important friends: Lady Charlotte Campbell, the Duke's younger daughter and Charlotte Clavering, the Duke's niece. After her mother's death in 1797, Ferrier assumed full responsibility for household management, looking after her father who lived until 1829. Ferrier did not marry. She enjoyed Edinburgh's polite social life and Walter Scott, whom she knew well and who was a younger colleague of her father's, described her as "simple, full of humour, and exceedingly ready at repartee, and all this without the least affectation of the bluestocking". In later life, Ferrier underwent evangelical conversion and joined the Free Church. From conviction she gave up writing fiction. Her eyesight was failing and she retired to private life. She died on 5th November 1854 and was buried in St. Cuthbert's Churchyard, Edinburgh.

Susan Edmonstone Ferrier

Scott's comment, and the fact that Ferrier herself gave up writing fiction latterly, show that polite society regarded novel-reading as a frivolous activity and regarded women, including writers, who could distinguish themselves intellectually, as rather off-putting. These social factors were very important in shaping the kind of fiction women wrote. **Marriage**, Ferrier's first novel, published anonymously in 1818, began as a joint project with Charlotte Clavering. Together they planned a novel which would "warn all young ladies against runaway matches". Ferrier was keen to justify her fiction by expressing responsible moral attitudes. "I expect it will be the first book every wise matron will put into the hand of her daughter," said Ferrier in a letter to Charlotte, embracing a didacticism which specifically countered the commonly-held view that novel-reading would corrupt women. **Marriage** was well received on publication. Although Charlotte did contribute a short section, she withdrew from the project and Ferrier herself completed the novel, which though didactic was also full of satire, humour and caricature. Lady Juliana elopes with a dashing Scots captain, Henry Douglas, to his Highland castle, Glenfern, where Juliana's life becomes more and more bewildering as she is exposed to a completely different culture. Unlike Scott's Romantic Highlands, Ferrier's can be coarse, poor and uncivilised, though she does admire the sturdy independence of character she finds there: Lady MacLaughlan is robust in speech and character and essentially good-hearted. Ferrier's didacticism and her ability to create strong women characters are echoed in the fiction of her contemporary Mary Brunton (1778-1818).

Ferrier wrote two subsequent novels, **The Inheritance** (1824) and **Destiny** (1831). The opening of **The Inheritance** echoes the opening of Jane Austen's **Pride and Prejudice**. Although Ferrier is sometimes compared with Austen, they take different approaches - Ferrier, a bold satirist; Austen, a sophisticated ironist. In her brilliant caricatures Ferrier is probably closer in spirit to Tobias Smollett, an earlier Scottish writer of satirical novels.

Beth Dickson

John Galt

Novelist.

John Galt

Galt was born in Irvine on 2nd May 1779. His family moved to Greenock when he was ten and he stayed there for the next ten years. He moved to London in 1804 and tried to establish himself in business with little success. From 1809 to 1811 he toured the countries of the Mediterranean and became acquainted with Lord Byron, of whom he wrote the first biography. He wrote plays, poetry and biography before discovering his real métier as a novelist. From 1827 to 1829 he acted as manager of a company engaged in the settlement of a large part of Ontario.

Some of his other works, especially his **Autobiography** and **Life of Byron**, are interesting, but Galt's main achievement lies in thirteen novels which are innovative, diverse, intelligent and highly entertaining. A group of them, which Galt called **Tales of the West**, are set mainly in the part of Scotland where he grew up: The Ayrshire Legatees (1820), **The Steamboat** and **Annals of the Parish** (1821), **Sir Andrew Wylie, The Provost, The Gathering of the West, The Entail** (1820), **The Last of the Lairds** (1826). Together they amount to a comprehensive picture of life in the world of Galt's youth and for a generation or two before, from about 1760 to about 1820. They make a brilliant use of Scots for dialogue and sometimes for narrative. Galt himself spoke of the Scottish people as fortunate in:

> *possessing the whole range of the English language as well as their own, by which they enjoy an uncommonly rich vocabulary.*

Even within this group of novels there is a remarkable range of techniques. **Annals of the Parish** and **The Provost** are what Galt called "theoretical histories", so accurate that they can be accepted as reliable accounts of social change. Both of these are narrated in the first person and are masterpieces of ironic self-revelation. **Sir Andrew Wylie** is on a larger scale and is one of the first novels to deal with politics and with murder and detection. **The Entail** is even more ambitious in its emotional depth and sense of tragedy.

Ringan Gilhaize (1823) is a powerful historical novel, heightened by a spirit of passionate identification with the Covenanters. **Lawrie Todd** (1830) and **Bogle Corbet** (1831) are among the first novels to be set in Canada and the United States. **The Member** and **The Radical** (1832) are ironic political novels reflecting the agitation for Parliamentary reform.

In 1834 Galt returned to Greenock and continued to write short stories with undiminished zest and humour. He died there on 11th April 1839.

Several of Galt's novels have stayed almost continuously in print and others have been rediscovered in recent years. Several are available in paperback. Among recent books about Galt are those by Ian A. Gordon (1972) and P. H. Scott (1985).

Paul H. Scott

Robert Garioch

Poet

Robert Garioch

Robert Garioch Sutherland (who wrote under the name of Robert Garioch) was born in Edinburgh on 9th May 1909 and was educated at the Royal High School and Edinburgh University. During the Second World War he served in the army in North Africa and was a prisoner-of-war in Italy and Germany from 1942 to 1945. He taught in schools in Edinburgh, London and Kent until he retired in 1964 and returned to Edinburgh. He was Writer in Residence at Edinburgh University, a "lexicographer's orraman" at the **Dictionary of the Older Scottish Tongue** and much in demand as a reader of his own poetry. He died in 1981. Sydney Goodsir Smith said of Garioch that he sat easily in the company of his predecessors, Ramsay, Fergusson and Burns. This is true particularly of Fergusson with whom Garioch felt a special affinity. They were both devoted to Edinburgh and were sharp-eyed observers of its life. Both wrote in Scots as a conscious effort to preserve the language and resist creeping Anglicisation and the reduction of Scotland to a province as a result of the Union of 1707. Garioch says in a poem addressed to Fergusson:

> *But truth it is, our couthie city*
> *has cruddit in twa pairts a bittie*
> *and speaks twa tongues, ane coorse and grittie,*
> > *heard in the Cougait*
> *the tither copied, mair's the pitie,*
> > *frae Wast of Newgate.*

Most of Garioch's work is in this "coorse and grittie" Scots which, as he said, he "used in the streets as a boy, but not at the R.H.S.". He wrote in a letter to J. K. Annand:

> *You and I belong to about the last age-group to have spoken*
> *Scots as laddies in the ordinary way of life … Perhaps not. But*
> *the great thing is that they keep on trying.*

It is a pungent language for the deflation of pomposity and pretension, but he also used the aureate style of the 15th century makars. He ranged from the comic to the philosophical, as in his long poem, **The Muir.**

Garioch wrote many verse translations, from the French of Apollinaire, the Greek of Pindar and Hesiod, the Latin of Arthur Johnstone and George Buchanan, including the latter's dramas, **Jephthah** and **The Baptist.** Above all he translated 120 sonnets of Guiseppe Belli, a Roman poet of the nineteenth century who was another kindred spirit.

His one book in prose, **Two Men and a Blanket** (1975) is a vivid and typically down to earth account of his experiences as a prisoner-of-war. Garioch's first publication, jointly with Sorley Maclean, was **17 Poems for 6d.** (1940). Several volumes of poetry followed, most of which were included in **Complete Poetical Works** (1983). **Jephthah and The Baptist** were published in 1959. Some of his letters and another play, **The Masque o' Edinburgh** (1954) appear in **A Garioch Miscellany**, edited by Robin Fulton (1986).

Paul H. Scott

Lewis Grassic Gibbon

Novelist, social historian & critic

Lewis Grassic Gibbon

James Leslie Mitchell was born in 1901 in Auchterless, but soon moved to Arbuthnott in the Mearns, countryside he was to make famous in his great trilogy **A Scots Quair** consisting of **Sunset Song** (1932), **Cloud Howe** (1933) and **Grey Granite** (1934). He was fortunate, like many Scots, in an early schoolmaster who recognised a precocious talent. His early experiences were diverse and unsatisfactory: he left school early, dabbled unsuccessfully in journalism, enlisted in the armed forces (which he hated) simply to survive in the Depression, though he was to travel to the Middle East and fire his imagination with the material of his first short stories which finally won him publication in the late 1920s.

A flurry of books marked the last half-dozen years of his life. Not everyone realised there were two authors producing a stream of material; there was a Scottish writer of great talent who called himself "Lewis Grassic Gibbon", a thin disguise of his mother's maiden name; there was a professional journalist and critic called "J. Leslie Mitchell" who kept an independent output of material just as professional, just as well written, but drawn from very different sources.

Mitchell believed whole-heartedly in the diffusionist theory that civilisation was a blight slowly strangling the native goodness and ability of human kind, the Depression simply the last gasp of a corrupt system, and that revolution and the shaking-off of Church and State, Government and class was the only way forward. A Marxist and an anarchist, Mitchell would have welcomed revolution, though as a writer he also faced a plangent nostalgia for a Scotland which he had known in youth, and watched destroyed by the First World War which changed the Mearns beyond recognition.

The themes of his work are clearly set. On the one hand, he produced autobiographical writing which celebrated that Scotland, **Stained Radiance, The Thirteenth Disciple,** an unfinished novel **The Speak of the Mearns** and — unforgettably — **Sunset Song** in which he shows his thinly-disguised autobiographical self (cleverly re-cast as a female protagonist, Chris, who runs through the trilogy as a binding thread) watching the sunset of an age, while singing its beauty as well as the harshness of the tough farming conditions of his childhood experience.

> *"…these were the Last of the Peasants, the last of the Old Scots folk."* says the minister as he unveils the war memorial to those who fell in the war: *"…never again will the old speech and the old songs, the old curses and the old benedictions, rise but with alien effort to our lips".*

In the first part of the trilogy we read about the author's childhood years, small farms, tight communities, harvest, spring, weddings, funerals — a Scotland easy to love, but never veering to kailyard or sentiment, since the other side is never far away, grinding repetitive work, gossip, spite. But the sunset comes with War, with the killing-off of the finest in the community, the dreadful stripping of the trees without which the old farming is effectively killed off.

The rest of the trilogy carries the story forward, away from nostalgia and times past, to a Scotland of here and now, industrial Scotland, smallish towns, finally the city (Aberdeen) in the Depression years, grey, hopeless, sometimes violent — a diffusionist's nightmare of the human spirit ground down. But it is a brave modern Scottish classic, turning away from easy temptations to romanticise Scotland, and facing up to the consequences of change. It was published in 1934, just before the author's death, and it was fully up to date.

Oddly enough, though much of the rest of his output was fantasy (highly successful science fiction, **Three Go Back** and **Gay Hunter**) it was firmly up to date too: Mitchell wrote about societies without the blight of civilisation, trying to show that human beings had once been free, could be again. Wonderfully successful short stories about the Scottish countryside make the same point again and again. Paradoxically, the author himself had to break free — to Welwyn Garden City, in Hertfordshire — to gain the freedom to see Scotland clearly. But when he did, he re-created the past, and sharpened the present, more successfully than any other writer of the century.

The Grassic Gibbon Centre

Part of the success lies in the use of language, innovative and very much open to first time readers. Without a strong covering of phonetic Scots, Mitchell writes in what looks like effortless English, though a lot of what is written can be read out aloud as Scots, many of the words disguised as common English words, though recognisable to a Scot for what they are. It is a non-threatening style, lyrical, musical, and it has done much to explain the success of his work. Television brought him to a new audience of millions, in North America as well as in Britain. He is widely taught in school and university. His Scotland is bitter-sweet, a place where real people live, and work, and die. It is not a Scotland of misty past, but a Scotland of sharp-edged present, with a respect for the past which does not sentimentalise or take refuge in a vanished countryside.

James Leslie Mitchell was to have a short success. Republished in the USA, he was rapidly growing in reputation when peritonitis carried him off suddenly in early 1935, at the threshold of what seemed likely to be a very successful career. His close friend Hugh MacDiarmid co-operated with him in **Scottish Scene** (1934), a jointly-authored squib in which they lambasted what was wrong with their country. In its savage attacks on people, institutions and cities (Mitchell on Glasgow and Aberdeen is unforgettable) it is elegant, witty, timely. It was a major loss to Scottish writing when Mitchell died, and thirty years of eclipse were to follow before the recent revival and — most important — republication which is again making available one of Scotland's most important modern authors.

In fulfilment of a long-standing local ambition to recognise his achievements the Grassic Gibbon Centre was established at Arbuthnott in 1991. It is open to visitors between April and October.

Ian Campbell

R B C Graham

Robert Bontine Cunninghame Graham
Travel writer & essayist

Robert Bontine Cunninghame Graham was born on 24th May 1852 in London where his father Major William Bontine was serving with the Scots Greys. By the time he died in Buenos Aires in 1936, Graham had travelled extensively in Europe, North and South Africa, and North and South America, gaining for himself the deserved reputation as a cultured, cosmopolitan hispanophile. However, by heritage, upbringing and temperament, he was *Scotissimus Scotorum*, and part of a complex genealogical tree that saw amongst his forebears many of the famous Grahams of Scottish history.

An inveterate letter-writer in his early travel adventures in Latin America, he began his literary life after the demise of his political career as a Radical M.P. (1886-92). Although Don Roberto, as his friends called him, is perhaps best known to many as a traveller and adventurer, a character, even an eccentric, he has left behind a solid corpus of some thirty books of sketches, biographies, histories and travel literature, not to mention translations, prefaces, pamphlets and other miscellaneous works.

When he did come to write his first work he treated matters close to home. **Notes on the District of Menteith** (1895), a travel guide "for tourists and others," is still a valuable vademecum for those who visit that beautiful misty area around the family home at Gartmore, and the Lake of Menteith. Graham's pithy remarks on the Scottish character, customs, history and other topics enable the book to transcend the purely regional.

Since **Notes on the District of Menteith** is the only full-scale book devoted exclusively to Scotland, Graham's reputation as a Scottish writer rests squarely on his Scottish sketches, some fifty out of a total production of two hundred, dating from **Father Archangel of Scotland** (1896) up through collections like **The Ipané, Success, Faith, Hope, Charity, Progress, His People, A Hatchment, Brought Forward, Redeemed, Writ in Sand**, and **Mirages**, his swan song published in 1936. In **The Scottish Sketches of R.B. Cunninghame Graham** (Scottish Academic Press, 1982) some attempt has been made to categorise these varied pieces, devoted to (i) landscapes and places, (ii) the Scottish character, (iii) scenes and situations, (iv) types and figures, (v) the Scots abroad (vi) Scottish stories. During his forty year career, one can also see a certain evolution from the first decade, against the excesses of kailyard sentimentality (e.g. in **The Ipané**, 1899). His middle period up to about 1916 (**Brought Forward**) represents the bulk of his work, with realistic portrayal of Scottish people and places. The third stage coincides with his support of Scottish nationalism (e.g. in **Redeemed**, 1927) and nostalgia for a heroic Scotland now gone.

When Don Roberto died in Argentina on 20 March 1936, he received a countrywide tribute from a people whose culture he also immortalised in his South American sketches, before his body was shipped home to be buried with his wife in the ruined Augustinian priory on the island of Inchmahome. The following year, June 1937, a monument to Graham was unveiled at Castlehill, Dumbarton, near the family home at Ardoch. In recent years it has been moved to Gartmore, closer to the other Graham estate. The last three decades have seen something of a revival of interest in this neglected writer.

John Walker

Kenneth Grahame

Essayist & children's writer

Kenneth Grahame, the third child of affluent parents, was born in Edinburgh on 8th March 1859. Shortly afterwards, the family moved to Inveraray, where his father was Sheriff Substitute. Grahame's father was a heavy drinker, incapable of caring for his family when Grahame's mother died. Kenneth was barely five. The children were sent to be brought up by relatives in Berkshire. Grahame was educated at St Edward's, Oxford but circumstances prevented him from following a university education in Oxford and he took up a position at the Bank of England, where he eventually rose to become the Secretary.

Kenneth Grahame

His first piece of published writing, **By a Northern Furrow**, appeared in 1888. Grahame continued to write articles and stories which were published in the **National Observer, St James Gazette** and the **Yellow Book** throughout the 1890s. **Pagan Papers** (1893) was based on some of these, including **The Olympians**, his child's view of the Victorian adult world. Grahame's **The Golden Age** (1895) received both critical and popular acclaim and centres on a fictional family created during his own childhood. The sequel, **Dream Days** (1898), featured the same five children, and was equally warmly received by the public. Many of the stories had already been published in journals.

In 1899 he married Elspeth Thomson and their only child, Alastair, was born in 1900. Grahame created Toad to amuse his young son, and many of Toad's early adventures are chronicled in correspondence. **The Wind in the Willows** was published in 1908 and, whilst it did not receive instant acclamation, its reputation grew quickly and it soon became a children's classic. The success of **The Wind in the Willows** rests on Grahame's wonderful characterisation of Toad, Rat, Mole and Badger and a combination of riverbank life, mouth watering picnics and outrageous adventures. The book's appeal was greatly enhanced by E. H. Shepard's delightful illustrations in the 1930 edition. A stage version, **Toad of Toad Hall**, was produced in 1930, dramatised by A. A. Milne. Obviously much of Grahame's original work was omitted but what was left was Toad's exciting adventures and it is widely accepted as a classic children's play. Other versions have appeared over the years, including Alan Bennett's stage version in 1991, and these have all helped to reinforce the public profile of the original work.

Grahame retired from the Bank of England in 1907, due to his ill-health. He continued to write and enjoy country life, particularly in Fowey, Cornwall. His son Alastair was tragically killed at the age of nineteen, following which Grahame and his wife spent long periods in Italy. Grahame did not write any other significant pieces. He died peacefully in 1932 at his home in Pangbourne.

Kenneth Grahame is best-loved and remembered for **The Wind in the Willows**, in which he used nature, the constant in his troubled childhood, to create a classic children's tale of characters familiar the world over.

Rhona Arthur

Elizabeth Grant

Diarist

Elizabeth Grant

Elizabeth Grant (1797-1886) of Rothiemurchus is so called to distinguish her from two namesakes: Elizabeth Grant of Carron (1745-1814)7 the song-writer, and Anne Grant of Laggan (1755-1838), who, like Elizabeth, also wrote about her experiences on Speyside. That the confusion should exist is understandable, but one suspects that the distinction between them might be better known. At least she is not known as Mrs Smith, although she married an Irish soldier of that name, and ended her days managing their estate in Ireland. Her father was an Edinburgh lawyer who inherited Rothiemurchus where Elizabeth, one of two brothers and three sisters, spent much time. He experienced considerable professional and financial difficulties until he became a successful judge in India. There Elizabeth met her husband, Colonel John Hay Smith.

Of several possible Grants, the **Oxford Companion to English Literature** chooses to mention only James Grant, the mid-century follower in Scott's footsteps. Elizabeth Grant was as interesting a writer as he was, and her work has lasted longer. She contributed stories and articles to journals just to earn money during her father's lifetime, but her fame rests almost entirely on her journal, written after 1845, and substantially edited and first published by her daughter in 1898.

What is appealing about Elizabeth Grant's **Memoirs** is that she describes early nineteenth century country life in the Highlands in the same intimate matter-of-fact way and with the same gentle wit as Jane Austen. Like Dorothy Wordsworth she was not writing for publication and this gives her work a refreshing honesty. One might suppose that life in the Highlands would be, in some way, more difficult and thus less sophisticated than life in the Home Counties, and so, perhaps, it was, but her account of it is of the same social, domestic and commercial concerns. Immortal characters, like Rob Roy and Niel Gow, and notable bits of scenery, like the Falls of Bruar, are introduced, not as set pieces, but as settings for everyday life.

The following extract illustrates her skills. She describes the perils of log bridges, but adds a telling anecdote about an elderly lady coming in the opposite direction:

> We were generally accompanied by an immense Newfoundland dog called Neptune, an especial favourite; he happened to be marching in front and proceeded to cross the log; on he stepped, so did the old woman, gravely moved the dog, and quietly came on the old woman, till they met in the middle. To pass was impossible, to turn back on the narrow footway equally so; there they stood, the old woman in considerable uncertainty. The dog made up his mind more quickly, he very quietly pushed her out of the way; down she fell into the stream, and on he passed as if nothing extraordinary had happened. She was a good old creature, just as much amused as we were, and laughed as heartily, and she spread the fame of Neptune far and near....

Elizabeth Grant died at Balliboys in Ireland. Her Scottish and Irish journals are available in admirable editions published by Canongate.

Louis Stott

Neil Miller Gunn

Novelist

Neil Gunn was born in Dunbeath, Caithness, on 8th November 1891, the seventh of nine children. His father, James Gunn, was a fisherman and his mother, Isabella Miller, a domestic servant. Gunn left Dunbeath in 1904 to live with his sister and her husband in St John's Town of Dalry, Kirkcudbrightshire. There he was privately educated in preparation for Civil Service exams which he passed in 1907. He moved to London experiencing the life of a rapidly expanding metropolis and being introduced to new political and philosophical thinking. In 1910 he became a Customs and Excise Officer and held a series of temporary Highland postings. During the First World War his duties routing ships around minefields exempted him from call-up. In 1921 he married Jessie Dallas Frew (1886-1963) known to her friends as Daisy, the daughter of an Inverness jeweller. They settled in Inverness when Gunn was appointed permanently to the Glen Mhor Distillery.

Neil Miller Gunn

Gunn published short stories throughout the 1920s and identified with Hugh MacDiarmid's aim of effecting a "renaissance" in Scottish literature. Gunn was friendly with such literary figures as Naomi Mitchison, Nan Shepherd, Eric Linklater and Edwin and Willa Muir. Though his play **The Ancient Fire** (1929) flopped it put him in touch with contemporary dramatists, James Bridie and John Brandane. J.B. Salmond, the editor of the **Scots Magazine**, and George Blake and George Malcolm Thomson, directors of the Porpoise Press, were Gunn's supportive publishers.

In the 1930s Gunn was closely involved in SNP politics in Inverness and was subsequently asked to serve on the Committee on Post-War Hospitals (1941) and the Commission of Inquiry into Crofting Conditions (1951). In 1937 after the publication of **Highland River**, Gunn felt sufficiently established to resign his job and live by writing. The strath where Kenn plays and the idea of exploring the river to its source provide him with an alternative education, sustaining him even during wartime. **Highland River** with its narrative innovations and "golden age" themes is a modernist classic.

Gunn's novels open with gloomy accounts of the effects of Highland economic stagnation in **The Grey Coast** (1926) and **The Lost Glen** (1928) but the memories of Dunbeath and its strath engender optimism in the lyrical **Morning Tide** (1931) and the mature **Highland River**. Highland life is explored historically in **Sun Circle** (1930), **Butcher's Broom** (1934) and **The Silver Darlings** (1941), set respectively in the time of Viking incursions, the Clearances and the prosperous herring fishings of the nineteenth century. The later fiction combines popular forms with universal themes. In the detective story **Bloodhunt** (1952), good triumphs over evil. In the dystopian **The Green Isle of the Great Deep** (1944), Highland values prevail over authoritarianism. These metaphysical themes, always present in Gunn's fiction, are inflected in later works by an interest in Zen Buddhism which he outlines in **The Atom of Delight** (1956), an unconventional autobiography.

Gunn was a great exponent of Highland life: **Whisky and Scotland** (1935) is the work of an aficionado; he enjoyed fishing and the companionship of those such as his brother John and his friend Maurice Walsh, who shared these interests. Neil Gunn died on 15th January 1973.

Beth Dickson

John MacDougall Hay

Novelist & journalist

John MacDougall Hay

John MacDougall Hay was born on 23rd October, 1880, in Tarbert, Loch Fyne, the son of Mary MacDougall and George Hay. He was educated at Tarbert High School and the University of Glasgow where he studied Natural and Moral Philosophy and English Literature. He graduated in 1900 becoming the headmaster of the Lionel Public School, Ness, Lewis. Later he moved to teach in Ullapool. There during a bout of rheumatic fever he decided to enter the ministry, returning to Glasgow to study divinity in 1905. He excelled in Church History and Biblical Criticism, winning class prizes. From his undergraduate days, he helped support himself by writing for newspapers and journals such as **MacMillan's Magazine, Chambers's Journal,** the **Spectator** and the **Glasgow Herald.** He was a student missionary at Morvern and then Assistant Minister at Govan Old Parish Church. In 1909 he was ordained and moved to a charge in Elderslie. On 28th October 1909 he married Catherine Campbell with whom he had two children: Sheena (b.1911) and George (b.1915); George Campbell Hay later became a distinguished Gaelic poet. After the publication of his first novel **Gillespie** in 1914 Hay considered leaving the ministry to take up a career in writing. He published another novel **Barnacles** (1916) and a poem **Their Dead Sons** (1918). A victim of poor health, he remained a parish minister until his death on 10th December 1919, aged 39. His funeral took place in Paisley Abbey.

Though its impact was blunted by the onset of the First World War, **Gillespie** has never entirely disappeared from view. It is loosely structured, includes some melodramatic lapses, but is punctuated with passages of astonishing descriptive power. It clearly echoes George Douglas Brown's **The House with the Green Shutters** (1901) in its structure and setting. Hay sets his action in a small, narrow minded community called Brieston, which is based on Tarbert. In his central character, Gillespie Strang, Hay unites Brown's John Gourlay and James Wilson, to produce someone who is financially astute but morally bankrupt and brutally materialistic. However, **Gillespie** differs from Brown's novel in many ways; particularly, it grapples with problems of acute religious doubt. Most of these are expressed in the terrifying nightmares of Gillespie's imaginative and spiritually sensitive son, Eoghan who desperately seeks some creed through which to critique his father. The Christ of the Gospels seems to offer him this, but Christ's ethic, though deeply attractive, seems powerless against the suffering which Brieston endures in the tragedy of the plague and at the hands of Gillespie. In **Gillespie** a weak Christ cannot modify the overwhelming presence of Fate which is the strongest spiritual reality in the novel, deriving its potency from the superstitious folk background of Eoghan's Highland grandmother. Fate cleanses but only at the terrible cost of the lives of all the main characters. It is the doctor who cares for the poor and the plague victims rather than the ministers whom the novel vindicates and in this is indicative of the move from a religious to a secular outlook which was to characterise the Scottish novel in the twentieth century.

Beth Dickson

Robert Henryson

Poet

Little is known about the life of Robert Henryson. He lived in the second half of the fifteenth century, and is thought to have taught at the grammar school attached to the Benedictine Abbey at Dunfermline. He was an educated man, but there is no record of his graduating from a Scottish university, and he may have studied abroad. In 1462 a "master Robert Henryson" was incorporated into Glasgow University as a bachelor in canon law; it seems possible that this was the poet, as is also the case with the notary of the same name who was active in Dunfermline in 1478. From an allusion in a poem by Dunbar we know that Henryson must have died before 1505.

Henryson excels as a narrative poet, although several short poems have been attributed to him. Two interesting but lesser works are **Robene and Makyne**, a humorous love-debate in the tradition of the French *pastourelle*, and **Orpheus and Eurydice**, a moralized interpretation of the classical myth. **The Testament of Cresseid**, however, is his masterpiece. Although it was prompted by a reading of Chaucer's **Troilus and Criseyde**, it is no mere sequel but a great and original poem in its own right. It tells the "tragedie" of Cresseid, after she has been abandoned by Diomede, and ultimately dies of leprosy. Her physical sufferings are vividly described, but Henryson is most concerned with Cresseid's spiritual and psychological development. He interweaves plot, symbol and imagery with great subtlety.

Henryson's most important other work is a collection of thirteen fables, usually entitled **The Morall Fabillis of Esope the Phrygian**. Some of the fables derive, ultimately, from those attributed to Aesop; but others originate in the beast-epic, a medieval cycle of stories associated with Reynard the Fox. Henryson handles the genre brilliantly. His skill at juxtaposing the different worlds of animals and humans is well illustrated in **The Two Mice**. One minute a character is a prosperous burgess, the next she shrinks into a mouse stealing cheese and oatmeal:

> The uther mous, that in the burgh can byde,
> Was gild brother and made ane fre burges ...
> And fredome had to ga quhair ever scho list,
> Amang the cheis and meill, in ark and kist [chest]. (Fables, 171 ff.)

In the Middle Ages fables were used for teaching purposes, and Henryson was conscious of the need for a "gude moralitie". Several fables receive an explicit spiritual meaning; others, such as **The Lion and The Mouse**, have veiled political implications. Henryson is a master of easy, colloquial dialogue, dramatic irony, witty proverb-capping, puns and other word play.

Although much admired by contemporaries, Henryson was largely forgotten in Scotland at the beginning of the seventeenth century, but in the twentieth century his reputation has soared.

The Poems of Robert Henryson, ed. Denton Fox, Clarendon Press, Oxtord, 1981.
John MacQueen, **Robert Henryson: a Study of the Major Narrative Poems**, Oxford, 1967.
Douglas Gray, **Robert Henryson**, Leiden, 1979.

Priscilla Bawcutt

Title page of "The Morall Fabillis of Esope the Phrygian".

James Hogg

Novelist & poet

James Hogg

Hogg was born in 1770 at Ettrickhall farm in the Ettrick valley: the cottage where he was born does not survive, but a Victorian monument marks the spot. His father, a sheep-farmer, became bankrupt in 1777, and as a result the young Hogg's formal schooling came to a premature end, the rest of his childhood being spent working as a cowherd and later as a shepherd. During his twenties, Hogg was employed as a shepherd by a relative of his mother's, Mr Laidlaw of Blackhouse farm, in Yarrow. At Blackhouse Hogg had access to a good collection of books; and he began to read widely, and also to write. Thereafter Hogg earned his living partly through various farming projects, and partly as a professional writer. In these roles he divided much of his time between Edinburgh and his native Ettrick Forest.

Hogg published mainly poetry until he was in his late forties. A particularly notable poem from this period is **The Queen's Wake** (1813), a book-length narrative in which the poets of Scotland assemble at Holyrood Palace for a bardic contest to celebrate the return of Mary Queen of Scots from France. A notable series of novels followed: **The Brownie of Bodsbeck** (1818); **The Three Perils of Man** (1822); **The Three Perils of Woman** (1822); **The Private Memoirs and Confessions of a Justified Sinner** (1824). An epic poem, **Queen Hynde**, followed in 1825: this is an exuberant and lively piece that is in essence Hogg's alternative version of James Macpherson's Ossian poem, **Fingal**. Many of Hogg's best later poems were collected in **A Queer Book** (1832).

Hogg's writings explore the supernatural with great power and sophistication, as in the **Justified Sinner**, which is regarded by many as the greatest of all Scottish novels. Equally powerful is **The Three Perils of Woman**, which explores the terrible aftermath of Culloden. **The Three Perils of Man** is Hogg's version of a Medieval romance. Overflowing with vivacity, this novel is full of devilry and witchcraft. Much of the action takes place at Aikwood in the Ettrick valley, where Gibbie Jordan witnesses a wedding between a demon and a witch. The happy couple retire to "a bower of the most superb magnificence"; and what happens next is later described by Gibbie to the King and Queen of Scots:

> … at length the lusty bridegroom, as I supposed, began to weary of his mate, for I saw the form of the bower beginning to change, and fall flat on the top, and its hue also become of a lurid fiery colour. I cannot tell your Majesties what sort of sensations I felt when I saw the wedded couple sinking gradually down through a bed of red burning fire, and the poor old beldame writhing to death in the arms of a huge and terrible monster, that squeezed her in its embraces, and hugged her, and caressed her till the spark of wretched life was wholly extinguished.

Aikwood Tower is now the home of Sir David and Lady Steel and a Hogg exhibition at Aikwood is open to the public during the tourist season. Current interest in Hogg is also reflected in the fact that a multi-volume edition of his Collected Works (prepared under the auspices of the University of Stirling and the University of South Carolina) is being published by the Edinburgh University Press.

Douglas S Mack

John Home

Dramatist

John Home

Home was born on 21st September, 1722, in Leith, where his father was town clerk. While a student of divinity at Edinburgh University he was involved in the '45 Rebellion as a volunteer on the Government side. He was captured after the Battle of Falkirk and imprisoned in Doune Castle, but escaped. Many years later he wrote **The History of the Rebellion in Scotland, 1745-6,** published in 1802.

In 1746, he became Minister of Athelstaneford, enjoying the patronage of Sir David Kinloch of Gilmerton House. According to his friend, the writer Thomas Carlyle, he had "not much wit, and still less humour", but had "so much sprightliness and vivacity that he was truly irresistible".

By 1749, he had written his first play, **Agis**, which was rejected by Garrick of Drury Lane, who also turned down Home's next work, **The Douglas,** declaring it "totally unfit for the stage". However, it was performed in Edinburgh in December, 1756, and took the place by storm, provoking the memorable audience cry: "Whaur's your Wullie Shakespeare noo?"

The Douglas was staged at Covent Garden in 1757 to great acclaim, but in June of that year, Home was forced to resign his parish, in order to prevent prosecution by the Presbytery who were outraged by his theatrical connections. His farewell sermon drew tears from his congregation. He went to London where he became private secretary to the Earl of Bute and in 1760 was awarded an annual pension from the Crown.

Meanwhile, **The Douglas** became an established success, though its greatest triumphs came in later years when Mrs Siddons played the role of Lady Randolph, declaiming pitifully to the young Douglas:

> *The love of thee, before thou saw'st the light*
> *Sustain'd my life when thy brave father fell,*
> *If thou shalt fall, I have nor love nor hope*
> *In this waste world! My son, remember me!*

Though not often revived after the mid nineteenth century, the play is still of considerable interest to students of dramatic and theatrical history.

Home produced six tragedies in all, though none of the others achieved the success of **The Douglas. The Siege of Aquileia** was performed at Drury Lane in 1760, but had only a short run. **The Fatal Discovery** staged in 1769, lasted only a fortnight. In 1773, his tragedy of **Alonzo** was performed at Drury Lane and proved a popular success, but **Alfred,** produced in 1778 and undoubtedly his weakest production, was a decided failure.

In 1767, Home had taken a lease on a farm at Kilduff in Athelstaneford, where he built a handsome villa. His declining years were spent in Edinburgh, and he died at Merchiston on 5th September, 1808. He was buried in South Leith churchyard where there is a memorial tablet erected by his nephew, John Home, W.S. A memorial pedestal surmounted by a bust of Home was erected in Haddington by public subscription in 1867 and now stands inside the church at Athelstaneford.

Veronica Wallace

Violet Jacob

Novelist, poet, short-story writer & diarist

The House of Dun

Violet Jacob was born Violet Kennedy-Erskine in 1863 at the House of Dun, her family's home near Montrose, now owned by the National Trust for Scotland ("Balnillo House" in her novel **Flemington**). The Erskine family history, which also fed into her fiction, was recorded by Jacob in **The Lairds of Dun** (1931). In 1894 she married Arthur Jacob, an Irishman serving in the British Army, and they went with his regiment to Central India. Violet Jacob's **Diaries and Letters from India 1895-1900** were published in 1990, illustrated with Jacob's own watercolours. The Jacobs were stationed for a time in Egypt, then lived in various parts of England, notably Shropshire and Herefordshire.

Jacob, whose mother was Welsh, set her first serious fictional work **The Sheepstealers** (1902) in the Welsh borders. This novel was well-received as was her next, the Angus-based **The Interloper** (1904), with its excellent Scots dialogue. In both works Jacob's prose is characteristically vivid and economical. Violet Jacob wrote books for children and several historical romances, but her most significant achievement is **Flemington** (1911; republished 1994). Set around the Jacobite Rebellion of 1745, this novel dealing with loyalty and betrayal can be placed in a tradition running through Scott and Stevenson. Archie Flemington, a young portrait painter and government agent, faces moral and emotional dilemmas when spying on James Logie, a Jacobite, who confides his own tragic history, and Archie, horrified:

> ... *looked round at the shortening shadows and into the stir of coming sunlight as a man looks round for a door through which to escape from impending stress. He, who was always ready to go forward, recoiled because of what he saw in himself.*

Archie finds himself torn between betraying James or his own political and family allegiances. Located in the symbolically suggestive landscapes of Angus, this novel, interweaving public and private history, is tragic and moving although lightened, like all Jacob's prose, by wit and dry humour. Jacob also published some fine short stories, mainly in **Tales of My Own Country** (1922), and **The Lum Hat and Other Stories: Last Tales of Violet Jacob,** edited by Ronald Garden, which appeared posthumously in 1982. Better known is Jacob's Scots vernacular poetry, in **Songs of Angus** (1915), **More Songs of Angus** (1918), **Bonnie Joann and Other Poems** (1921), **The Northern Lights and Other Poems** (1927), and collected in **The Scottish Poems of Violet Jacob** (1944). Her poems appeared in Hugh MacDiarmid's **Northern Numbers** (1920-21) and John Buchan's **The Northern Muse** (1924). Recent critics appreciate the serious and radical as well as the sentimental elements in her poetry, which draws on ballad and folk song. **Tam i' the Kirk** is often anthologised, but poems like **The Baltic, Craigo Woods, The Jaud** and **The End o't** are also interesting. **The Wild Geese** has been set to music by Jim Reid.

The heaviest blow in Violet Jacob's life was the loss of her only son, Harry (born 1895), at the Battle of the Somme in 1916. After her husband's death in 1937, Jacob returned to Angus where she died in 1946, having received an honorary degree from Edinburgh University in the previous year.

Carol Anderson

James Peebles Ewing Kennaway

Novelist & screenwriter

Kennaway was born in Auchterarder, Perthshire, on 5th June 1928 into a comfortable middle-class family. His father was a solicitor and factor and his mother Marjory was a doctor. When he was only twelve James's father died, a fact which he was later to claim tainted much of the rest of his life.

James Peebles Ewing Kennaway

Educated at Glenalmond, he did his National Service in the Cameron Highlanders and later with the Gordon Highlanders on the Rhine, whom he remembered for their "petty squabbling for authority in the mess". This period was to form the basis for his first, and most memorable novel, **Tunes of Glory**. At Oxford, he studied politics, philosophy and economics, and toyed with the idea of politics as a career before gradually realising that he wanted to write. He joined a London publisher and married an Oxford student, Susan Edmonds.

Kennaway's first literary success came with the publication of the short story **The Dollar Bottom** in **Lilliput** in 1954. Two years later he published **Tunes of Glory**. An apparently simple but tense novel, it revolves around rivalry, a theme that, in many forms, dominated all Kennaway's fiction. It is the tale of conflict between the tough, acting colonel, Jock Sinclair, and Basil Barrow, a public-school product, trained at Sandhurst, who nominally takes charge. The two vie for supremacy in bleak Scottish barracks which are clearly modelled on Kennnaway's own first military home, the Queen's Barracks in Perth. The opening paragraph of the novel is an accomplished piece of storytelling:

> *There is a high wall that surrounds Campbell Barracks, and in the winter there is often a layer of snow on top of it. No civilian rightly knows what happens behind that grey wall but everybody is always curious, and people were more than ever curious one January a year or two ago.*

A taut and moving tragedy, it drew great plaudits, winning praise even from such notoriously anti-Scottish critics as Evelyn Waugh who admitted that it revealed "a powerful natural talent which may well develop into something important". It was later made into a compelling film, starring Alec Guinness.

Although he devoted himself now to writing, Kennaway never matched the success of his first novel. Subsequent works include the novels **Household Ghosts** (1961), **Some Gorgeous Accident** (1967) - which was largely based on his own experience of infidelity, following his wife's affair with David Cornwall (the novelist John Le Carré) - and **The Cost of Living Like This** (1969), which each played with triangular sexual relationships. Despite the overtly Scottish provenance for many of his stories, Kennaway distanced himself from Scotland and insisted that he was a "writer from Scotland" referring disparagingly to the country as "a bad society".

After a spell in Hollywood writing scripts Kennaway returned to writing novels or film adaptations of his books. Increasingly volatile in his personal life, he was haunted by his father's early death, wishing to cram as much experience as possible into a short space. His fear was prophetic. He died at forty, on 21st December 1968, when he suffered a coronary while driving. His posthumously published novel **Silence** is regarded by some as equalling **Tunes of Glory** in quality, but remains far less well known.

Rosemary Goring

Jessie Kesson

Novelist & playwright

Jessie Kesson

Jessie Grant Macdonald was illegitimate, born in the workhouse in Inverness in 1916 and brought up in the backwynds of Elgin. "The lane was home and wonderful". When her mother contracted syphilis Jessie was moved in 1924 to Proctor's Orphanage, near Skene, Aberdeenshire, "a cold place for the heart". These childhood experiences form the basis of her novel **The White Bird Passes** (1958), later televised by the BBC. The novel is eloquent about Jessie's anguish at being separated from her mother, who for all her problems was still a figure redolent with magic and whose love of music and literature was the source of her daughter's unique literary talents and determination to be a poet and writer.

Deprived of the university education she craved, she left the orphanage in 1932 to go into service, but suffered a nervous breakdown. Sent to a croft near Loch Ness she met Johnnie Kesson, a cattleman, whom she married in 1934. The couple had a son and daughter. Abreachan was the backcloth for **The Road of No return** a story in **Where the Apple Ripens** (1985).

Johnnie's career took them to Rothienorman which formed the setting for **Glitter of Mica** (1963) and during the war to the Black Isle where the presence of Italian prisoners gave the idea for the novel and film **Another Time, Another Place** (1983).

In 1940 her poem **Fir Wud** caught the attention of Neil Gunn and she became a contributor to **The Scots Magazine**. Encouraged by Nan Shepherd she entered a short story competition which she won, and this was followed by an invitation to write for BBC Aberdeen, over 30 features and plays subsequently being broadcast.

Jessie Kesson lived in London from 1947, the move being essential to permit her to write unfettered by temptation of the Kailyard. She carried her country with her "Morayshire...the heart, Aberdeenshire...the mind" and it was with enormous pride that she accepted honorary degrees from the Universities of Aberdeen and Dundee in the 1980's. She eked out a living as a cleaner, artist's model and social worker, but her main work was writing. She produced **Women's Hour** and also wrote over ninety plays for radio and TV, notably **You Never Slept in Mine**.

Jessie Kesson's writing was of the highest quality, pared to poetic essence. **The White Bird Passes** in its story of Janie is a triumphant poetic tale of a spirit that poverty cannot diminish. **Glitter of Mica** relays the changing fortunes of the isolated parish of Caldwell as seen through the tragic story of the Riddel family, while the stories in **Where the Apple Ripens** depict those who haunt the fringes of society, the old, the homeless, the lonely.

Jessie Kesson combined regional interests with larger themes and although adopting Scottish idiom and character her writing is universally accessible. She gave a genuine voice to the experiences of women and painted an honest depiction of the rigours of life. It is her authenticity, her earthy humour, her extraordinary memory and intellect, her deep feelings for her childhood and the human condition that make this author outstanding and important to the development of Scottish writing. Jessie Kesson died in London on 26th September 1994.

Alistair Campbell

Andrew Lang
Scholar & man of letters

Andrew Lang

Andrew Lang, born in Selkirk in 1844, died in Banchory in 1912. He is a well-respected alumnus of St Andrews University where one of his early pieces imagined Dr Johnson on the links. He spent much of his active professional life in London, but he had a considerable knowledge of much of Scotland, and an appreciation of the Scottish character which illuminated his work, and, at the end of his life, led him to begin the influential **Highways and Byways of the Border,** completed by his wife and son. What Lang singularly failed to do was to write either a lasting novel or a really striking poem, but he was a very significant literary figure. His column in **Longman's Magazine** did much to form literary opinion in the late nineteenth century. His contemporaries included Stevenson, whom he often encouraged and almost collaborated with, and George Douglas Brown whom he brought to public notice. Lang's interests were diverse and his expertise considerable. He wrote many elegantly put together books which were, and are, a delight to read. His intellect and his wit can perhaps be best appreciated in **Adventures Among Books**. A Snell exhibitioner at Balliol, he became a fellow of Merton College, Oxford, and a distinguished classical scholar whose versions of the **Odyssey** (1879), and the **Iliad** (1882), are still highly regarded. Like Stevenson, whom he first met there, he went as an invalid to the Riviera, and his first book of poems was **Ballads and Lyrics of Old France** (1872). He wrote the narrative poem **Helen of Troy** (1882), published four other books of poetry and two novels, **The Mark of Cain** (1886) and **The Disentanglers** (1902). Of his poems **Waitin' for the Glasgow Train** and **The Fairy Minister** are sometimes remembered.

His "Borders" edition of Scott has not been surpassed, his biography of Lockhart was exemplary, and he sought to emulate Perrault and the Brothers Grimm in the field of British Folklore. He undertook wide-ranging anthropological research, published in such books as **Custom and Myth** (1884), **Myth, Literature, and Religion** (1887), and **The Making of Religion** (1898). He adapted many well-known fairy stories in the **Blue Fairy Book** (1889), followed by several other such books for children. He also revived one of the fundamental treatises of Scottish folklore, Robert Kirk's **Secret Commonwealth**. He published this and other books about folklore in collaboration with Alfred Nutt who, like Lang, was a leading figure in the Society for Psychical Research, and the Folklore Society.

Compton MacKenzie characterised his **Pickle the Spy** as infuriating, but essential reading for any scholar who wished to comprehend the Jacobites. This sums Lang up: his work was rarely the product of completely original scholarship, he was, at times, slapdash, and he allowed his own opinions (always interesting) to intrude into works which perhaps ought to have been more even-handed. His substantial **History of Scotland** (1900-07) was an idiosyncratic, yet intriguing book. Lang deserves a place as an important Scottish writer.

Louis Stott

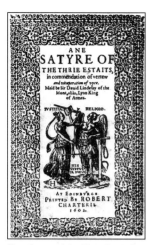

"Ane Satyre of the Thrie Estaits", title page, 1602.

Sir David Lindsay

Poet & playwright

Sir David Lindsay (c.1486-1555) came of a land-owning family in Fife, and throughout his life was closely associated with the Scottish court. His earliest work, **The Dreme** (1528), contains an affectionate account of James V as a child, and Lindsay's care of him.

Some time before 1530 Lindsay became a herald, an office that took him on diplomatic missions to France and England, and involved him in court entertainments, pageants, and other ceremonial duties. By 1542 he had received a knighthood and later became Lyon King of Arms. After James V's death he continued in royal service during the Regency of Mary of Guise, and died early in 1555.

Although Lindsay was a prolific poet, there is no evidence that he started writing until his forties. His shorter poems are intimately concerned with the court: **The Deploratioun** (1536) is a formal elegy for James's first queen, Madeleine; others, such as **The Complaint**, **The Testament of the Papyngo**, and **The Complaint of Bagsche**, are satires, attacking the vices of greedy courtiers and worldly churchmen. Lindsay's tone towards the King himself is lightly jesting, but often admonitory and remarkably outspoken. Stylistically, these works owe much to Dunbar and other earlier Scottish poets.

Lindsay's undoubted masterpiece is **Ane Satyre of the Thrie Estaitis**, a political morality play. This seems to have existed in two forms: a version for indoor performance at court (c.1540), and a much longer version designed for public performance out of doors, at Cupar in 1552 and at Edinburgh in 1554. In structure the play drew upon the traditions of medieval drama, but Lindsay's target was contemporary society: the corruption of the King's councillors, the dishonesty of craftsmen, and the superstition and greed found in all sections of the church. The play voiced a passionate appeal for the reform of the Scottish church and state:

> *Get up, thou sleipis all too lang, O Lord,*
> *And mak sum ressonabill reformatioun! (1160-61)*

Whether Lindsay was wholly committed to the Protestant cause, however, is much debated. The play is dramatically effective: it consists of a series of lively, sometimes farcical scenes, couched in vivid and trenchant dialogue.

To Lindsay's last years belong two very different works: **The Monarche, or Ane Dialogue betwix Experience and ane Courteour**, is a weighty account of world history; **Squire Meldrum** is a verse biography of a friend, cast in the form of a chivalric romance.

For several centuries Lindsay was by far the most popular of early Scottish poets, largely because he was perceived as a champion of Protestantism. Today he is remembered chiefly for **Ane Satyre of the Thrie Estaitis**, which has had many performances since its successful revival at the Edinburgh Festival of 1948.

The Works of Sir David Lindsay, ed. Douglas Hamer, 4 vols. Scottish Text Society, Edinburgh, 1931-1936.

Carol Edington, **Court and Culture in Renaissance Scotland: Sir David Lindsay of the Mount**, East Lothian, 1995.

Priscilla Bawcutt

David Lindsay

Novelist

David Lindsay was born in Blackheath, London, on 3rd March 1876, and brought up there, though he spent holidays with his father's relations near Jedburgh. Since his father deserted the family at an early stage, financial difficulties prevented Lindsay from going on to university. Instead, in 1894, he began work in an insurance office, remaining in this job for over twenty years. He married in 1916 and moved from London to the country, where his wife encouraged him to become a full-time writer.

Lindsay's first novel, **A Voyage to Arcturus**, was published in 1920, but sold fewer than 600 copies. A surrealist fantasy drawing to some extent on the work of George MacDonald, it has always been known as a complex and difficult book, though a recent critic maintains that a reader who approaches it with sympathy "will find the experience both profound and astonishing". The central character, Maskull, travels to the planet of Tormance, a satellite of Arcturus. The planet is controlled by the evil Crystalman, but alongside this world exists another one, Muspel, and "Crystalman's empire is but a shadow on the face of Muspel". Maskull's adventures begin as a quest for Surtur, whose drums he has heard on Earth. (The critic quoted above, J. B. Pick, suggests elsewhere that the reader should not so much search for the meaning of the book as "hear the drumbeats"):

> *He heard what sounded like the beating of a drum on the narrow strip of shore below. It was very faint but quite distinct … He now continued to hear the noise all the time he was lying there. The beats were in no way drowned by the far louder sound of the surf, but seemed somehow to belong to a different world.*

A Voyage to Arcturus, though unsuccessful during Lindsay's lifetime, is now recognised as an important work both in Scottish literature and in the fantasy genre. Acknowledged by C.S. Lewis as a major influence on his own fantasy novels, it has recently been reprinted in the Canongate Classics series. Canongate has also republished Lindsay's second novel, **The Haunted Woman** (1922), also a fantasy but with a terrestrial setting, which has been described as better written, though slighter, than **A Voyage to Arcturus**.

Before his death in Hove on 16th July 1945 Lindsay published three further novels, leaving two more, **The Violet Apple** and **The Witch,** in manuscript form. These were posthumously published in 1976. His work is now attracting considerable critical attention, for instance in J. B.Pick's **The Great Shadow House** (1993) and Colin Manlove's **Scottish Fantasy Literature** (1994), both of which deal with **A Voyage to Arcturus** at some length, and in Bernard Sellin's **The Life and Works of David Lindsay** (1981).

Moira Burgess

Book Jacket for David Lindsay's novel "Sphinx".

Eric Linklater

Eric Linklater

Novelist

Although Eric Linklater was born in Penarth, Wales, in 1899, he spent much of his childhood in Orkney and considered himself an Orcadian. He was educated at Aberdeen Grammar School, but his medical studies at the University of Aberdeen were interrupted by nightmarish service as a sniper with the Black Watch in World War I. After the War, he graduated in English Literature and took up journalism, becoming Assistant Editor of **The Times of India,** 1925-27. There followed two years in the USA as a Commonwealth Fellow, from which emerged the work which established his reputation as a humorist, the novel **Juan in America** (1931), which satirised Prohibition America with immense vigour.

In all, Linklater was to write twenty three novels, ranging from the Viking saga of **The Men of Ness** (1932) to the Cold War fable **A Spell for Old Bones** (1949), from the dramatic retellings of Biblical stories **Judas** (1939) and **Husband of Delilah** (1962) to the anti-war comedy **Private Angelo** (1946). The novels all possess an amazing command of language, but if there is among this diversity a common theme, it is that all feature a central character in search of contentment.

In 1933, he married Marjorie MacIntyre, and then stood as a candidate for the National Party of Scotland in a by-election, thinly disguising the unsuccessful campaign in the farcical **Magnus Merriman** (1934), notable for its merciless guying of stalwarts of the Scottish Literary Renaissance, in particular MacDiarmid.

During World War II, he commanded Fortress Orkney as a Major in the Royal Engineers, then worked for the War Office recording the Italian Campaign, rediscovering the hidden art treasures of Florence - he kissed Botticelli's **Primavera**. His humane gentle story about Private Angelo, the Italian peasant who finally finds courage, is one of the finest novels of the War.

Throughout the fifties and sixties Linklater continued to add to his impressive range, following the moving prose-poem **Roll of Honour** (1961) with the knockabout exposure of charlatanism **A Man over Forty** (1963) and the experimental Pythonesque fantasy **A Terrible Freedom** (1966). Simultaneously he found time to write plays for radio and (less successfully) for stage; some thirty short stories which for range and depth rival those of any Scottish author, collected as **The Stories of Eric Linklater** (1968); and many works of travel, history, biography, criminology, military history and children's fiction. There are three volumes of autobiography, **The Man on my Back** (1941), **A Year of Space** (1953), and **Fanfare for a Tin Hat** (1970), which must be supplemented by Michael Parnell's fine critical biography **Eric Linklater** (1984). Parnell apart, only Francis Russell Hart in **The Scottish Novel** has written at any length on Linklater's work, a reminder of the deplorable narrowness of Scottish (and British) literary criticism.

Eric Linklater died on 7th November 1974 and is buried in Harray Kirkyard, Orkney.

John MacRitchie

John Gibson Lockhart

Novelist & biographer

John Gibson Lockhart was born in Cambusnethan in Lanarkshire in 1794, and received his university education (like his friend and contemporary John Wilson, "Christopher North") at Glasgow and Oxford. Like Wilson, he settled in Edinburgh, one of a circle of bright young Tory lawyers, alert, intelligent, well-read and mischievous. The launching of **Blackwood's Edinburgh Magazine** in 1817 was a golden opportunity for their talents, and Lockhart and Wilson took over the ailing magazine after half-a-dozen dull issues and transformed it in October 1817 into the most shocking (and best-selling) review of its time. The lampooning of contemporary writers (particularly Keats and Leigh Hunt) is savage caricature, the deliberate practical jokes and mystification, and the bad-taste parody of the **Chaldee Manuscript** (a not very opaque description of contemporary Edinburgh in Old and New Testament language) hard to defend. Right or wrong, Lockhart and Wilson (with the help of Hogg among others) catapulted **Blackwood's** to the head of critical writing, alongside the Whig **Edinburgh Review**, and made themselves considerable national literary figures. The partnership was to last till 1825, when Lockhart was tempted to London to edit the **Quarterly Review**.

This apart, Lockhart was a writer of considerable merit. Like his future father-in-law Walter Scott he was keenly interested in German literature, and translated Schlegel; independent of Wilson, he wrote **Peter's Letters to his Kinsfolk** in 1819, a fictional account of a visit to Lowland Scotland, describing the great men he met in innocent terms whose satire was easily interpreted by those in the know. The book remains one of the most engaging introductions to the Edinburgh of the time.

Lockhart's solid achievement as a writer is twofold. One is as a novelist, with **Valerius** (1821), **Adam Blair** (1822), **Reginald Dalton** (1823) and **Matthew Wald** (1824) to his credit. The other is as biographer, with lives of Burns (1828, the inspiration of Carlyle's immortal essay on Burns), Napoleon (1829) and, most importantly, Scott in 1837-8. Lockhart was close to Scott from his marriage to Sophia Scott in 1820, and very close at Scott's death. He was close, too, to Scottish country religious life (the son of a minister) and his enduring fictional success lies (in **Adam Blair**) in probing the psychology of a country minister in a sexual predicament. When Adam, a widower (his name no coincidence) is tempted by the visit of an old friend — now a married woman estranged from her husband — to solace his loneliness, he falls prey to temptation and for one night of pleasure imposes on himself a heavy and lifelong burden of guilt and penance. The novel breaks new ground in honestly asking what pressures the ministry brings, and endures. If the sexual content is stunted and if it ducks many questions, it remains an impressive attempt to open a taboo subject.

Lockhart died in 1854, having for many years divided his life between London and the Borders. He died in Abbotsford, and is buried, fittingly, at Dryburgh Abbey.

Ian Campbell

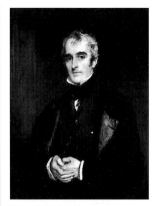

John Gibson Lockhart
by Sir Francis Grant

Fionn Mac Colla

Novelist & historian

Fionn Mac Colla

Fionn Mac Colla, the pen-name of Thomas Douglas MacDonald, was born in Montrose in 1906 and died in Edinburgh in 1975. On leaving school, he trained as a teacher in Aberdeen and taught briefly in Wester Ross before accepting a lectureship in the Scots College at Safed in Palestine. Returning to Scotland in 1929 with the intention of going to University, he started writing seriously, and his first novel **The Albannach** was published to critical acclaim in 1932. In 1940 he was appointed to a teaching post in Benbecula, thus beginning a sojourn of over twenty years in the Western Isles, mostly in Barra. He returned latterly to Edinburgh, retiring from teaching in 1967.

Mac Colla saw the Scottish condition mirrored in his own family background, in which his father's Black Isle and Glenmoriston forebears represented the Gaelic element in the equation, and his mother's folk, who came from the Mearns, the Scots element. He joined the National Party of Scotland in 1928, and remained a life-long nationalist. He was born into a Plymouth Brethren family, but rejected that creed as an adult. Later, he and his wife Mary became converts to Roman Catholicism. In politics, religion and life he sought an integration of consciousness which is a *Leitmotiv* in his writing.

Mac Colla's philosophy as a writer is under-pinned by a knot of ideas and ideals: Scotland's unity as a nation was forged in the Wars of Independence; that unity was challenged by powerful political-economic interests, especially from the sixteenth century onwards; these were permitted to flourish by a negative force which has dogged Scotland since then; the negative force is a function of political emasculation and the workings of Calvinism on the Scottish mind, which has to be confronted before Scotland can be a wholesome place.

In **The Albannach** the Highlands are the backdrop for the story of Murdo Anderson, who experiences the spiritual, social and economic constraints of contemporary Scotland, before finding a sort of salvation through returning to his home village and rekindling community spirit and local tradition there. In **And the Cock Crew** (1945) Mac Colla took the "story" back a stage, to the time of the Highland Clearances, where again the opposition between the teaching of the Presbyterian Church and the spirit of the community is an important axis. Although he did not complete the major novel he planned for the Reformation period, two chapters appeared separately - as **Scottish Noel** and **Ane Tryall of Heretiks**. Like all his historical writing, they show tremendous assurance in handling the past, both in historical accuracy and in realism. He is a highly accomplished writer whose representations of dialogue show a great sensitivity to linguistic variation past and present, while his descriptive passages are equally well executed.

Fionn Mac Colla's literary output was relatively small, but he is a major figure of the Scottish Renaissance. Many of his ideas about Scotland, Scottish history and Scottish writing have been echoed by subsequent writers with a variety of political outlooks but it required a special courage and obduracy to articulate them in the years before the decline of Empire and the Church.

William Gillies

Hugh MacDiarmid

Poet

Hugh MacDiarmid was born Christopher Murray Grieve on 11th August 1892 in Langholm, Dumfriesshire. He derived much of his future radicalism from his father, a rural postman, and from the fiercely independent tradition of the burgh. At Langholm Academy he was taught by Francis George Scott, the composer who was later to set to music so many of his lyrics. When Grieve was a pupil-teacher in Edinburgh his literary abilities were encouraged by George Ogilvie, whose advice he sought and generally accepted over many years. After the death of his father, in 1911, Grieve turned to journalism. He served in the RAMC from 1915 to 1920, and eventually found himself in 1921 editor-reporter of the **Montrose Review**.

In Montrose he threw himself into the political life of the community, and from Montrose he edited and published the three issues of **Northern Numbers**, representative collections of contemporary Scottish poetry, and a remarkable series of periodicals, of which the first was the most important. **The Scottish Chapbook** proclaimed its editor's belief in the possibility of a great Scottish Literary Renaissance; its motto was "Not Traditions—Precedents".

It was in the first number of the **Chapbook** (August 1922) that Hugh MacDiarmid made his appearance, as the author of a semi-dramatic study, **Nisbet**, but the third number printed a poem by Hugh MacDiarmid, **The Watergaw**, which had already appeared anonymously the month before in an article of Grieve's in the **Dunfermline Press**.

Hugh MacDiarmid

Grieve's first original book, **Annals of the Five Senses** (1923), was also published from the author's home in Montrose. It is dedicated to John Buchan, who two years later provided the preface to MacDiarmid's first volume of poetry, **Sangschaw**. A perceptive reviewer recognized that MacDiarmid was writing:

> *…in the belief that Scotland still has something to say to the imagination of mankind, something that she alone among the nations can say, and can say only in her native tongue.*

A Drunk Man Looks at the Thistle, which is generally considered the poet's greatest achievement, appeared in 1926. Here exquisite lyrics are integrated into the erratic progression and glorious illogicality of the drunk man's wayward thought.

While MacDiarmid was writing and publishing these poems Grieve was contributing to the **Scottish Educational Journal** a notable series of articles. These **Contemporary Scottish Studies** gave a new perspective on the literary scene in Scotland, attacking almost every respected member of the establishment. They were published as a book in 1926, and fifty years later were reprinted by the **Journal** with the "furious and fascinating" correspondence they had immediately evoked.

MacDiarmid's **First Hymn to Lenin**, a poem which greatly influenced the English poets sympathetic to Communism: Auden, Spender, and Day Lewis, was published in 1931. In that same year Grieve's wartime marriage ended in divorce. His second marriage, to Valda Trevlyn, began a partnership that endured. The Grieves moved in 1933 to the Shetland island of Whalsay, which was their home for the next nine years.

Surmounting the difficulties of poverty and remoteness MacDiarmid produced in 1934 three important books: a miscellany, **Scottish Scene**, in collaboration with Lewis Grassic Gibbon; a collection of essays, **At the Sign of the Thistle**; and a further volume of poems, **Stony Limits,** in which he moved towards a new use of English. In 1936 **Scottish Eccentrics** appeared, of which a friend commented that the book's glaring omission was a final chapter on C. M. Grieve; and in 1939 **The Islands of Scotland**, an idiosyncratic look at the Hebrides, Orkney, and Shetland. MacDiarmid's most individual and unusual autobiography, **Lucky Poet: A Self-Study in Literature and Political Ideas** (1943), is a fascinating and heady mixture of prose and poetry, chaotic and irritatingly repetitive, but stimulating and full of interesting ideas: a unique book.

Grieve/MacDiarmid published in all some thirty major books, and he left traces of a number of unfulfilled projects, "intentions subsequently abandoned or subsumed in other works". Of these the most important is the prodigiously long poem, **Mature Art**, of which parts were published as **In Memoriam James Joyce** (1955) and **The Kind of Poetry I Want** (1961). The "as-yet-unpublished third volume" was to be called **Impavidi Progrediamur**, later given the Scots title, **Haud Forrit**.

MacDiarmid's poems in Scots range widely both in form and in imaginative intensity: there are the deceptively simple, the humorous, the powerfully realized, the hauntingly beautiful, the richer linguistically, such as **Water Music** (one of his many tributes to James Joyce), and the later, austere Shetland lyrics in **Stony Limits**. In **Stony Limits**, too, in English, we find poems of political protest and propaganda along with the linguistic experiments, and the profound meditation, **On a Raised Beach**, and such gems as the well known quatrain, **The Little White Rose**, with its echo of Yeats, another of his contemporaries with whom MacDiarmid stands comparison.

MacDiarmid's later poetry may well be the kind he wanted, but not all his readers can readily accept the lengthy cataloguing of prosaic facts, the interminable quotations, the scientific data, the contradictions, yet in this "strong solution of books" we are always conscious of the poet at work and in control.

MacDiarmid is a difficult poet, but he can also write simply and directly, just as the man who could be so vitriolic and opinionated an adversary was also one of the kindliest and most generous of friends.

The Grieves had moved in 1951 to a cottage near Biggar, and this was the poet's home until his death on 9th September 1978. He was buried in Langholm, where a memorial sculpture now stands.

A reader coming to MacDiarmid's poetry may well be daunted by the 1500 pages of the two-volume **Complete Poems**, edited by Michael Grieve and W. R. Aitken, but there is an excellent introduction in the **Selected Poems**, edited by Alan Riach and Michael Grieve. Another guide to the essential MacDiarmid is **The Thistle Rises**, an anthology of his poetry and prose, edited by Alan Bold, who also edited MacDiarmid's **Letters** and wrote the definitive biography, **MacDiarmid**. There is a carefully annotated edition of **A Drunk Man Looks at the Thistle** by Kenneth Buthlay. Scotsoun has produced a number of recordings of the poems.

An ambitious project to publish or republish MacDiarmid's complete works is now in progress, with Alan Riach as general editor.

W R Aitken

George MacDonald

Novelist, poet & preacher

George MacDonald

MacDonald was born in Huntly on 10th December 1824, but moved soon after with his family to a nearby farm. He went to university in Aberdeen in 1840 and to Highbury College in 1848 to train as a Congregational minister. He was forced to resign from his first charge at Arundel in 1853 and lived thereafter as a man of letters and on the charity of his friends and disciples.

His first important original publication was a long religious poem, **Within and Without** (1855) but a more important landmark was **Phantastes** (1858), his first major contribution to the genre of fantasy and a complex attempt to communicate that sense of otherness which is his abiding concern in his writing. Influenced by both English and German Romantic writers, and by religious poets of the Renaissance, **Phantastes** with its poetry and its visionariness was in turn an important influence on C. S. Lewis and his circle. Here, its hero starts a new day after a night at the foot of a protective beech:

> *I must act and wander. With the sun well risen, I rose, and put my arms as far as they would reach around the beech-tree, and kissed it, and said good-bye. A trembling went through the leaves; a few of the last drops of the night's rain fell from off them at my feet; and as I walked slowly away, I seemed to hear in a whisper once more the words: "I may love him, I may love him; for he is a man, and I am only a beech-tree."*

MacDonald produced fantasy writing for both children and adults throughout his long career. A large family and no steady income, however, forced him to more saleable works and in 1863 he published **David Elginbrod,** the first of around two dozen novels. In it he gave expression to his belief in universal redemption, a theological outlook which was still a minority view in the middle of the century but which became more accepted by the end of MacDonald's life. Half of these novels are set wholly or partly in nineteenth century Scotland and they form one of the most important fictional treatments of the Scottish scene between the generation of Scott and his circle, and the time of Stevenson.

A friend and confidant of "Lewis Carroll" and of John Ruskin, MacDonald survived many years of ill-health, partly by wintering abroad (often in Bordighera) during his later years. He died in Ashtead, Surrey on 18th September 1905. A memorial to him was recently erected in Drumblade Churchyard, Aberdeenshire. There has been a revival of interest in his writings and ideas, both here and abroad, in the last twenty years, though only his classic books for children remain securely in print.

Roland Hein, **The Harmony Within: The Spiritual Vision of George MacDonald**, Grand Rapids, 1982.
William Raeper, **George MacDonald**, Tring, 1987.
David S Robb, **George MacDonald**, Edinburgh, 1987.

David S Robb

Duncan Ban Macintyre

Poet

The monument to Duncan Ban Macintyre near Dalmally.

Duncan Ban Macintyre, Donnchadh Ban Mac an t-Saoir, was born in Glenorchy in 1724 and died in Edinburgh in 1812. In 1746 he was present at the Battle of Falkirk about which he wrote a humorous poem. He lost his sword at the battle in which he fought though perhaps not with great conviction on the Government side against Prince Charles. The poet never learned to read or write and had to trust to his memory for the reproduction of his own compositions. The Rev Donald MacNicol, minister of Lismore, helped with the transcription of the poems.

Though Duncan Ban wrote many poems including **Oran an t-Samhraidh** (Summer Song), satires, love songs and drinking songs, his most memorable work is in the poems he wrote about the Argyll-Perthshire borders, and about the deer in the glen of which he was gamekeeper. The chief of these poems is **Moladh Beinn Dobhrain** (The Praise of Ben Doran). This is a wonderful poem of fidelity of description and love of the deer, of the food they eat, of the guns that shoot them and the dogs that harry them:

Honour past all bens
to Ben Doran
of all beneath the sun
I adore her

The poem has a happy sunny atmosphere and there is no doubt that this period was the most joyful and creative of Duncan Ban's life. Unlike Wordsworth, he does not philosophise about Nature nor does he sentimentalise the deer. His other famous Nature poem is **Oran Coire a Cheathaich** (The Song of the Misty Corrie) where he deals with the natural description of the corrie, grasses, berries, flowers, birds, trees, bees and so on.

In 1767 Duncan moved to Edinburgh and became a member of the City Guard (a sort of policeman) and served in the Breadalbane Fencibles. He composed prize poems on Gaelic and the bagpipes in 1781, '82, '83, '84, '85 and '89. In 1789 he competed with Donald Shaw for the post of Gaelic Bard to the Highland and Agricultural Society, but was not successful though his poem was highly commended. He retired from the City Guard in 1806, and six years later he died in Edinburgh, and was buried in Greyfriars Churchyard. It can be said that his true inspiration lay in the country, and it did not bloom in Edinburgh.

A monument to the poet marks his grave in Greyfriars Churchyard and another stands south of Dalmally overlooking Loch Awe.

Hugh MacDiarmid has translated **Ben Doran** and so has Iain Crichton Smith whose translation can be found in his **Collected Poems** (Carcanet, 1992). A number of Duncan Ban's poems can be found translated in Professor Derick Thomson's **Gaelic Poetry in the Eighteenth Century - A Bilingual Anthology** (published by the Association for Scottish Literary Studies, 1993). They include a part of **Ben Doran**, **Summer Song** and **Song of the Misty Corrie**.

Duncan Ban's reputation remains high and surely **Ben Doran** will remain as one of the great poems in Gaelic, musical, fertile, sunny and joyful.

Iain Crichton Smith

Sir Edward Montague Compton Mackenzie

Novelist & journalist

Sir Compton Mackenzie

Mackenzie was born in West Hartlepool on 17th January 1883, the son of an actor, Edward Compton. His birth was entered in the parish register under his father's family name of Mackenzie but throughout his life he was always known to his friends as "Monty".

Following his education at St Paul's School and Magdalen College, Oxford Mackenzie studied for the English Bar but he was attracted both by the theatre and by the possibility of earning his living from writing. The publication of his first novel **The Passionate Elopement** (1911) confirmed his promise but it was not until the arrival of **Sinister Street** (1913) that he achieved substantial literary success. Thinly autobiographical, it followed the low-life adventures of its hero, Michael Fane, in London and Oxford and it won warm praise from writers as different as Henry James and Scott Fitzgerald.

Having established himself as one of the leading writers of his generation Mackenzie embarked on a dazzling literary career which covered fiction, travel, biography, essays, poetry and journalism. During the First World War he served on the Gallipoli front and worked for British intelligence in Greece. The experiences produced two volumes of war memoirs and a novel, **Extremes Meet** (1928).

After the war he lived on the Mediterranean island of Capri and entered his most prolific period. Between 1937 and 1945 he published the sextet, **The Four Winds of Love** which follows the life and loves of John Ogilvie, one of his most enduring heroes. He also wrote two entertaining accounts of lesbian love, **Vestal Fire** (1927) and **Extraordinary Women** (1928).

In 1934 Mackenzie built a house called Suidheachan at Northbay on the island of Barra in the Outer Hebrides and committed himself to the cause of Scottish nationalism. After the Second World War he wrote a series of enjoyable and finely observed comedies of Scottish life, the most successful of which was **Whisky Galore** (1947), a fictional account of the sinking of a ship laden with whisky on the island of Eriskay. As with the equally entertaining **Rockets Galore** (1957) it was made into a successful film. In all his novels Mackenzie's fiction is characterised by his ability to produce farcical plots and spirited dialogue.

Mackenzie's later years were dominated by the production of the ten volumes of autobiography, **My Life and Times** (1963-1971). By then he was living in Edinburgh at 31 Drummond Place in the city's Georgian New Town which was to be his home for the rest of his life. He died on 30th November 1972 - St Andrew's Day - and was buried at Eoligarry on the island of Barra. During the brief burial service his old friend Calum Johnston collapsed and died after playing a lament on the bagpipes.

By the time of his death much of Mackenzie's earlier work had been largely forgotten but his Scottish novels have retained their appeal and **The Four Winds of Love** is rightly regarded as a major contribution to Scottish fiction.

Trevor Royle

Henry Mackenzie

Novelist & Essayist

Henry Mackenzie

Son of a doctor, Mackenzie was born in Edinburgh on 26th July 1745. He was educated at the High School of Edinburgh and the University there. His legal apprenticeship began in 1761 and in 1765 he was admitted Attorney in the Court of Exchequer in Scotland. As a leading taxation attorney he regularly visited London, becoming a close friend to many prominent lawyers and politicians of the day.

Mackenzie first achieved publication in 1763 with a poem in the **Scots Magazine**. A number of verses and romantic ballads followed, including **Kenneth** and **Duncan**, both later included in Herd's **Ancient and Modern Scottish Songs, Heroic Ballads, Etc.** (1776):

> *For I have stuid whar honour bade,*
> *Though death trade on his heel:*
> *Mean is the crest that stoops to fear;*
> *Nae sic may Duncan feel.*

Mackenzie's biographer, H.W. Thompson, wrote:

> *Here, if he had known the young poet had his feet on the pathway of Romance; before him was the lordly road which Walter Scott was to tread, but he chose to turn aside into the little lane of Sensibility.*

In 1771, he published the novel for which he is best known. **The Man of Feeling** is a sentimental story; its hero, Hartley, possesses an ideal sensitivity, displayed as feelings of virtue, pity, sympathy and benevolence. As innocence and weakness are deceived and exploited, the hero's response, and the intended response in the reader, is copious shedding of tears of sympathy and charity.

The Man of Feeling was an immediate success, and the title came to be attached to the author himself. Burns wore out two copies and called it "a book I prize next to the Bible". Mackenzie published two other novels in the same sentimental vein: **The Man of the World** (1773) and **Julia de Rubigne** (1777). Through these novels, his plays and editorship of the journals **The Mirror** and **The Lounger**, Mackenzie established himself as a leading member of Edinburgh's literary society.

The issue of **The Lounger** of 9th December 1786 contained his paper discussing Burns' Kilmarnock Edition. In this first important criticism of Burns, Mackenzie praised "this heaven - taught ploughman", and assured his success in Edinburgh. Significantly, it was Burns' English language poems which attracted his particular favour.

He was instrumental in founding the Royal Society of Edinburgh (1783) and the Highland Society of Scotland (1784). Mackenzie chaired a committee of the latter which investigated the authenticity of the Ossian poems "translated" by James Macpherson. As a man of letters Mackenzie aspired to improve Scottish literary taste. In dedicating **Waverley** to Mackenzie, Scott describes him as "our Scottish Addison".

He died on 14th January 1831 and was buried in Greyfriars Churchyard, Edinburgh.

Alan Reid

Ian Maclaren

Novelist

"Ian Maclaren" was the pseudonym used for fiction writing by John Watson, who was born in Manningtree, Essex, on 3rd November 1850. The family moved to Perth in 1854, and Watson was educated at Edinburgh University and the Free Church of Scotland college in Edinburgh. Ordained as a Free Church minister, he spent some years in Logiealmond, Perthshire, and in Glasgow, before beginning a long career in Liverpool.

He published a number of religious works under his own name, but as Ian Maclaren was a leading member of the Kailyard School of Scottish fiction which came into being towards the end of the nineteenth century. Maclaren's first work in this genre, **Beside the Bonnie Brier Bush** (1894) takes its title from Burns: "There grows a bonnie brier-bush in our kail-yard ... "

Beside the Bonnie Brier Bush is a collection of "idylls" or stories, set in the fictional village of Drumtochty. The village is thought to be based on Logiealmond, where Maclaren began his ministerial career, but the picture of rural life, in common with most Kailyard works owes more to nostalgia than to the reality of Maclaren's time, or perhaps of any time. The narrator, though he may be a returned exile, is an "outsider" by virtue of his education and experience, so that he is able to observe the simple Scots-speaking villagers from a somewhat patronising height. Church affairs are at the centre of Drumtochty life, and the climax of a story is often a pious deathbed scene, where a brilliant young man or a saintly veteran goes to his eternal reward.

> *It was a low-roofed room, with a box-bed and some pieces of furniture, fit only for a labouring man. But the choice treasures of Greece and Rome lay on the table, and on a shelf beside the bed College prizes and medals, while everywhere were the roses he loved. His peasant mother stood beside the body of her scholar son, whose hopes and thoughts she had shared, and through the window came the bleating of distant sheep.*

The Kailyard School has attracted much unfavourable criticism over the years for its sentimentality and its perceived misrepresentation of Scottish life, but some re-evaluation has recently taken place. Gillian Shepherd's essay **The Kailyard** in **The History of Scottish Literature,** vol. 3 (Aberdeen University Press, 1988) supplies a balanced view of Maclaren and the other Kailyard authors, with a useful reading list.

Maclaren's other works of fiction, which include a second collection of stories, **The Days of Auld Lang Syne** (1895), and the novel **Kate Carnegie and Those Ministers** (1896), generally follow the Kailyard formula, and were extremely popular in their day, selling well in both Britain and America. Maclaren, a gifted preacher, became sought after as a public speaker, and was on his third lecture tour of America when he died in Mount Pleasant, Iowa, on 6th May 1907.

Moira Burgess

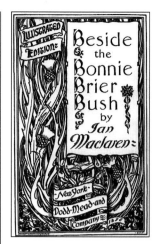

"Beside the Bonnie Briar Bush" title page.

Alistair MacLean

Alistair MacLean

Novelist

MacLean was born in Glasgow in 1922. A son of the manse, he spent his early years in Daviot, near Inverness. Educated at Hillhead High School, Glasgow, he worked in a shipping office before joining the Royal Navy at the outbreak of the Second World War. He served on the Russian convoys, in the Aegean and the Far East, and his experiences in the navy provided the background for his early novels.

After the war MacLean attended Glasgow University, graduating in 1947. He began teaching English in Gallowflat School, Rutherglen and began writing short stories, some of which were published in **Blackwood's Magazine**. At the age of 32 he entered a short story competition in **The Glasgow Herald**, which he won with a story entitled **The Dileas** receiving a prize of £100.

Ian Chapman, an editor with Collins, was so impressed by the story he asked MacLean to attempt a novel. He received the manuscript of **HMS Ulysses** ten weeks later. The novel drew heavily on the author's experiences of the Russian convoys and became one of the most successful British novels of all time, selling 250,000 hardback copies within six months. This success was followed by **Guns of Navarone**, and **South By Java Head**, both of which later became films, and MacLean's reputation was established. He was a master of pace, often at the expense of characterisation, keeping the action moving so that the reader had no time to stop and think.

MacLean's relationship with his publisher, Collins, was not always an easy one, and to prove that it was not his name alone that was selling his books, he produced in 1960 **Dark Crusader** under the pseudonym of Ian Stuart, followed by **Satan Bug** in 1961 which became a successful film. In the mid 1960s Elliot Kastner, a film producer/director, persuaded MacLean to turn his hand to screenplays and this resulted in **Where Eagles Dare**, which had great success as a film.

In all, MacLean produced fourteen screenplays including **Breakheart Pass** and **Heritage Tower**, some of which were subsequently turned into novels, although some critics felt that the screenplay/novels lacked the power of his early work. Throughout his career he produced twenty seven books, mainly adventure stories, but he also wrote a biography of Captain Cook in 1972.

In his later years his personal life became increasingly shambolic, and his addiction to alcohol undermined his health. Jack Webster, in his biography of MacLean, felt that:

> *... if escape was a prime characteristic of his fiction it was no less a feature of his own life. He was searching for greater meaning and fulfilment while running away from the chances of finding it.*

Alistair MacLean died in February 1987 in Munich and was buried in Celigny, Switzerland. It has been said that MacLean wrote to a formula:

> *A hero, a band of men, hostile climate, a ruthless enemy and, as often as not, a Judas figure who almost upsets the mission.*

If it was a formula, it was an extremely successful one, eighteen of his books selling over a million copies.

Robert Craig

Robert McLellan

Playwright, poet & short story writer

Robert McLellan was born at Kirkfieldbank, Lanarkshire in 1907. His childhood, spent on his grandparents' farm, inspired the **Linmill** stories (collected 1977) which are told from the perspective of a child and written in Scots. From 1938 until his death in 1985 McLellan lived on Arran, which provided the setting for the long dramatic poem **Sweet Largie Bay** (1956), and **Arran Burn** (1965) written for a BBC television programme about the island.

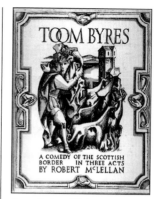

Cover design of Robert McLellan's play "Toom Byres".

It is as a playwright that McLellan is best known. Influenced by Hugh MacDiarmid and the Scottish Literary Renaissance movement, McLellan always wrote in the Scots tongue about Scottish subjects and characters. The use of Scots is one of the most notable features of McLellan's writing. He emphasized that he used a living spoken language not an anachronistic artifact. In performance the lively theatricality of the dialogue communicates with an audience but a glossary is often helpful to a reader. One play, **The Flouers o' Edinburgh** (1948), focuses on a debate between eighteenth century Edinburgh gentlemen about the conversational use of Scots or English. From his treatment of one character who abandons his "barbarous" native tongue it is clear that McLellan favours the use of Scots.

Although nearly all of his plays have an historical setting McLellan's view of history avoids sentimentality and, even though many of them are comedies, focuses on a harsh believable world. It is the individual, both historical and fictional, who interests McLellan as a way of exploring Scottishness. In his best known play, **Jamie the Saxt** (1937), James VI is shown to be a statesman who, in spite of the threats to the crown, his own life and the stability of the state, manages to triumph through an unheroic combination of luck, folly, tenacity and cunning. At the end of the play James looks forward to the Union:

> *Aa that I hae wished for is promised at last! … the dream o my life come true! It gars my pulse quicken! It gars my hairt loup! It gars my een fill wi' tears! To think hou the twa pair countries hae focht and struggled. … And then to think, as ae day it sall come to pass, that I Jamie Stewart, will ride to Londan, and the twa countries sall become ane.*

In a later play, **The Hypocrite** (1967), by placing the action in eighteenth century Edinburgh and therefore beyond libel action, McLellan is able to ridicule the outraged reaction of some people to a "happening" at the 1963 Edinburgh Festival where a naked girl was fleetingly glimpsed above the speakers' platform at a conference. The play also suggests that such reactions are not always as innocent as they seem.

Robert McLellan's plays are about Scotland and the Scots character but they are never simply parochial. He explores Scottish themes in the tradition of the medieval makars like Henryson and Dunbar and, using a mixture of farce and history, he deals with major issues like religion, the divine right of kings and the rights of ordinary citizens.

Chris Ravenhall

James Macpherson

Poet & translator

James Macpherson

James Macpherson was born in Ruthven, Badenoch on 27th October 1736 and attended both Aberdeen and Edinburgh Universities before returning to his native district as a teacher. By 1758 he had moved to Edinburgh where he worked as a tutor and tried to make his name as a poet.

Celticism was then in vogue through the "discovery" of Welsh bardic poetry. The excitement generated by a Gaelic ballad published in the **Scots Magazine** in 1756 may have spurred Macpherson to similar activity. In 1760 he published **Fragments of Ancient Poetry,** which gave glimpses of a rugged, ancient land inhabited by venerable warriors brooding on past glories.

> *Son of the noble Fingal, Ossian, Prince of men! What tears run down the cheeks of age? What shades thy mighty soul?*
>
> *Memory, son of Alpin, memory wounds the aged. Of former times are my thoughts; my thoughts are of the noble Fingal.*

These "translations" gave Macpherson a success his original compositions had not achieved. Having claimed that the "fragments" represented larger works still obtainable, he was encouraged to collect more. Before long Macpherson published his main works, **Fingal** and **Temora**: verse translations (or so he claimed) of epic poems by Ossian, commemorating the exploits of a warrior race flourishing in Scotland in pre-Christian times.

The success of these works was phenomenal. Innumerable editions in most European languages bear testimony to the magic of their elemental landscapes and the proud, melancholy men who haunted them. Comparisons with Homer were frequent. However, there was also controversy, since some critics accused Macpherson of forgery and deception. The debate took on political overtones and continued throughout Macpherson's lifetime, and still colours people's attitudes towards Macpherson, and towards Gaelic poetry.

In truth, there were no third-century Gaelic epics preserved, even fragmentarily, by eighteenth century tradition-bearers. There were, however, orally preserved heroic ballads in which larger-than-life characters (including Fionn and Oisean) repelled invaders and had adventures in stylistically distanced, linguistically archaic verse. Reminiscences of this poetry are embedded in Macpherson's texts, and he perhaps saw himself as reconstituting epics from fragmentary remains. Yet much of the poetry is his own, and his "learned" commentaries are disingenuous.

Opinions vary as to Macpherson's literary standing. Distaste for his deception has loaded the dice against him, as have our contemporary preferences for the realism of Gaelic folk-poetry. However, Macpherson's influence on European literature (e.g. on Goethe and the German Romantics) is undeniable.

Macpherson himself took little part in the controversy after its initial exchanges, in which he clashed famously with Dr Johnson. In 1764 he was preferred to an administrative post in Florida. In 1766 he returned to England, where he lived in considerable comfort as a historian, lobbyist and pensioned Government propagandist. In his last years he returned to Badenoch, where he died in 1796. He was buried, at his own direction, in Westminster Abbey.

William Gillies

Gavin Maxwell

Writer & naturalist

Gavin Maxwell (1914-69) has a distinctive place in the succession of British writers who have communicated a passion for the environment in a way that surpasses mere description. He may be mentioned in the company of Gilbert White, of W. H. Hudson, and of Edward Thomas. His lifestyle and his love of nature might be more readily accepted now than it was, indeed he might have fitted more comfortably into any other age than the years following the Second World War. His great book, **Ring of Bright Water** (1960), brought him enormous literary success, yet it described a life doomed to destruction.

His grandfather, Sir Herbert Maxwell, was a fine topographical writer, but Gavin Maxwell's books enjoyed a much more universal success, perhaps because he combined his eye for nature with impossible dreams and a determination to live life in his own way which he communicated in elegant, readable prose, close, at times, to poetry. Maxwell was a manic-depressive minor aristocrat, both talented and charming, but selfish. He might have been a diplomat; he strove to be an explorer, a shark-fisherman, a painter, and a poet. Although handicapped he served as an instructor with SOE in the Highlands during the war.

His first book **Harpoon at a Venture** (1952) described a characteristic Maxwell enterprise: commercial shark fishing from Soay in Skye (1945-48). The enterprise failed partly because it was undercapitalised, and partly because the sharks were more elusive than he supposed they might be. However, the book established his love affair with the Hebridean seas, and his career as a writer. His books are essentially about places: his description of the Marsh Arabs of Iraq in **A Reed Shaken by the Wind** (1957) has a distinctive position in the literature of exploration, and was hailed by the **New York Times** as "near perfect". As he had accompanied one of the most famous Arabian explorers, Ernest Thesiger, who also wrote in the same genre, this was praise indeed.

In all Scotland there is nowhere more evocative of a particular author and a specific book than Sandaig where his ashes were scattered and there is a memorial to Edal, his otter. He disguised its name he said, not because it is difficult to find, but because such places should stay in the imagination. After the success of **Ring of Bright Water** - the unforgettable title, which Maxwell did not acknowledge, is from a poem by Kathleen Raine - he was inundated with visitors with no respect for his privacy, but nowadays it must resemble the place which fired his imagination. **The Rocks Remain** (1963) is a darker sequel, and **The House of Elrig** (1965) describes his passion for his calf-country, Galloway where he was born.

In **Gavin Maxwell - A Life** (1993) Douglas Botting, a latish member of Maxwell's entourage, has written a fine biography, perceptively dealing with his tempestuous relationship with Kathleen Raine and many others, including Peter Scott and Richard Frere, and faithfully bringing this exasperating, but exhilarating person to life.

Louis Stott

The Gavin Maxwell memorial, The Raiders Road, Galloway.

Hugh Miller

Geologist, journalist, newspaper editor & folklorist

Hugh Miller

Miller was born in Cromarty, Easter Ross, on 10th October 1802, in a cottage still preserved by the National Trust for Scotland. His father Hugh, a ship's captain, was lost at sea in 1807, and the influence of his superstitious mother Harriet gave him a strong sense of the supernatural which lasted all his life. A wild and unruly boy, he preferred wandering the nearby beaches to attending school, and his formal education ended in a fight with the schoolmaster. At seventeen he was apprenticed to a stonemason, a craft which led directly to his interest in fossils. Later his health was affected by the arduous life of a mason, and he turned to a career in writing.

He published a book of poems in 1829, but had more success with some articles in the **Inverness Courier** on the herring fisheries. In 1835 he published **Scenes and Legends of the North of Scotland.** This collection of tales is still an important source of local history and folklore, and shows Miller's story-telling abilities at their best. He combines accurate description of the real world with marvellous flights of imagination, for example in recounting a woman's dream of walking on the bottom of the ocean:

> *I walked as light as ever I had done on a gowany brae, through the green depths o' the sea. I saw the silvery glitter o' the trout an' the salmon shining to the sun, far, far aboon me, like white pigeons i' the lift; and around me there were crimson star-fish, an' seaflowers, and long trailing plants that waved in the tide like streamers …*

In 1839 he moved to Edinburgh to become editor of **The Witness,** a newspaper established to oppose the Patronage Act, which allowed landowners to appoint Church of Scotland ministers over the heads of local congregations. A staunch Presbyterian, Miller was a leading figure in the Free Church after the Disruption of 1843. He wrote hundreds of articles on every subject, attacking social injustices such as child labour and the Highland Clearances. His bestselling introduction to geology, **The Old Red Sandstone,** was published in 1841, and was followed by **Footprints of the Creator** and **The Testimony of the Rocks,** in which he tried to reconcile his religious beliefs with the scientific evidence of his studies.

My Schools and Schoolmasters (1854), is a very readable memoir of his early years, intended to show ordinary working-class people that they could improve their circumstances by self-reliance and reading. He himself was a famous figure in Victorian Britain, but, overworked and suffering from stress, he committed suicide on 24th December 1856.

He is buried in Grange Cemetery, Edinburgh, and an imposing monument was built to his memory in Cromarty. Dickens, among others, praised him as "a delightful writer, an accomplished follower of science, and an upright and good man", but his reputation suffered because he had opposed the theory of evolution. As a journalist and folklorist, however, his writing is still fresh and entertaining.

James Robertson

Edwin Muir

Poet & novelist

Born in 1887 in Orkney, in childhood Edwin Muir experienced "Eden" before, aged fourteen, encountering the "fallen" world when circumstances forced his family to move to Glasgow. In four years, death seized both parents and two of Muir's five siblings, deepening his sense of the gulf between the Orkneys and the city and causing a nervous perturbation which shadowed his life and shaped his work.

By 1919, Muir had married Willa Anderson, a happy partnership recorded in her loving memoir **Belonging** (1968), and moved to London where persisting psychological distress led him to Jungian analysis. A vision in which he was witness to the Creation inspired him fully to engage in his own "creation" as a poet. Indeed, experience made him see human life in such terms, individual "story" re-enacting archetypal "fable", loss of childhood innocence a reworking of man's expulsion from Eden.

Edwin Muir

His world is full of paradox, good co-existing with evil, living with dying, love with hate, leading to images of journeys, of roads, of labyrinths:

> *There is a road that turning always*
> *Cuts off the country of Again.*

Time looms large, pregnant with intimations of death:

> *Time with his hour glass and his scythe*
> *Stood dreaming on the dial...*

whilst the poet suffers the strangeness of it all, invoking images of agrarian childhood:

> *Can we till these nameless fields,*
> *Nameless ourselves, between the impotent dead*
> *And the unborn...*

and feels alienated even from himself:

> *Packed in my skin from head to toe*
> *Is one I know and do not know.*

In addition to seven collections of poems (1925-1956), now published together in **The Complete Poems of Edwin Muir** (1991), Muir wrote three novels (1927 -1932), with Willa translated Kafka and taught in Europe before coming in 1935 to St. Andrews, where he produced his controversial assessment of Scottish culture **Scott and Scotland.** Attacking what he had once approved of, "synthetic Scots" as used by MacDiarmid, Muir's thesis was that while Scotland was torn between Lallans and English, she would fail to produce great literature.

In English and in conventional verse forms Muir expressed the emotions of one who saw fable in every story and timelessness all-pervasive. Unhappiness at exile from Eden and life amid paradox finally left Muir in 1950 when, as recalled in **An Autobiography** (1954), he became Warden of Newbattle Abbey and found peace by inspiring its adult students.

Muir died in 1959 and is buried near Cambridge; a memorial seat in the Pentland Hills recalls Muir's achievements.

Mary Ross

Neil Munro

Neil Munro

Novelist, poet & journalist

Munro was born in Inveraray on 3rd June 1863, the illegitimate son of Ann Munro, kitchen-maid. Rumour identifies his father as a member of the Ducal house of Argyll. Educated at Inveraray School, at thirteen he started work in the office of the Sheriff-clerk of Argyll. He moved south in 1881 to follow a career in journalism, eventually becoming assistant editor of the **Glasgow Evening News.**

A short story collection, **The Lost Pibroch,** appeared in 1896 and his first novel **John Splendid** was published in 1898. This and his other historical novels, such as **Doom Castle** (1901), deal with Munro's constant theme - the impact of change on the Highlands. **The New Road** (1914) is perhaps his most accomplished work in this genre and contains a chilling portrayal of evil in Simon Fraser of Lovat. Set in 1733, General Wade's new military road is both central to the plot and a metaphor for the changes that contact with the English-speaking south must bring to the Gaelic north. Munro, a Highlander in exile, lamented these changes, while recognising their inevitability and their benefits. His young hero Æneas MacMaster reflects on the military road:

> It means the end of many things, I doubt, not all to be despised, - the last stand of Scotland, and she destroyed. And yet, and yet, this New Road will some day be the Old Road, too, with ghosts on it and memories.

Around 1902 Munro retired from full-time journalism, retaining a commitment to produce a weekly column for the **News.** This column was to win him as much fame as his novels. In it appeared three series of humorous short stories, **Archie, my droll friend; Jimmy Swan, the Joy Traveller** and above all - **Para Handy**. These last, the adventures of a West Highland puffer skipper and the crew of the coaster *Vital Spark* have enjoyed continuing popularity and have been adapted for television, stage and film. Munro used these stories for light-hearted social comment on contemporary events such as the introduction of old age pensions. Munro thought little of journalism, or of these pieces, which he published as "Hugh Foulis" to distance them from his serious works.

During the 1914-18 War Munro returned to full-time journalism and suffered the loss of his son, Hugh, on the Western Front. His later output was slight. A volume of poetry appeared after his death, as did two volumes of collected journalism.

Munro died, in Helensburgh, on 22nd December 1930. He is buried in Kilmalieu Cemetery, Inveraray and a monument to his memory was unveiled in Glen Aray in June 1935. Although awarded the Freedom of Inveraray and honorary doctorates by Glasgow and Edinburgh Universities and described as "the apostolic successor of Sir Walter Scott", Munro's reputation suffered a posthumous decline, the consciously archaic and poetical style of the novels undoubtedly playing a part in this. There has, rightly, been a resurgence of interest in Munro and his major works are again available.

Brian D. Osborne

Charles Murray

Poet

Charles Murray was born in Alford, Aberdeenshire on 29th September 1864. After schooling in Alford he trained as a civil engineer in Aberdeen. He emigrated in 1888 to South Africa and became a partner in a firm of architects and engineers. In his self-imposed exile he took to writing verse as he strove to maintain strong links with his family and his native Alford. He wrote in the local vernacular to please his father. Eager to see his verses in print he had twelve copies of **A Handful of Heather** printed privately in Aberdeen in 1893, only to withdraw it and to discard all but thirteen of the forty poems it contained. These were revised and published later in **Hamewith**. In 1895 he married Edith Rogers. They had three children, one son and two daughters. WIth the outbreak of the Boer War in 1899 he served in the Railway Pioneer Regiment. He also served in the First World War.

Charles Murray

His home in Scotland and the language of his childhood were still his inspiration and the publication in 1900 of **Hamewith**, meaning "homewards" makes his motivation clear. **Hamewith** was re-published five times during his life. Its recurring theme was life in the Vale of Alford and its language was the broad Scots of the farming folk. From 1901 Murray's career flourished and he held various senior appointments in the Transvaal before becoming Secretary of Public Works, South Africa in 1910. A new edition of **Hamewith** was published in London in 1909 with an introduction by Andrew Lang who wrote:

The Scots of Mr. Murray is so pure and so rich that it may puzzle some patriots whose sentiments are stronger than their linguistic acquirements.

He noted also that Murray's translations of Horace into Scots, "are among the best extant." Still another treasure in **Hamewith** is **The Whistle**, a poem full of humour and high spirits:

He blew them rants sae lively, schottisches, reels and jigs,
The foalie flang his muckle legs an' capered ower the rigs.

His poems in **The Sough o' War** published in 1917 demonstrate yet again the poet's fervour for his own countryside and his pride in the courage of his countrymen. With **In the Country Places**, published in 1920, Murray's wry humour and deep insight had full scope in poems like, **Gin I was God** and **It wasna his Wyte**.

It was coorse still an' on to be walloped like thon,
When it wasna his wyte he was late.

Murray became LLD (*honoris causa*) of Aberdeen University in 1920 and honoured as CMG in 1922.

He died in Banchory on 12th April 1941. His ashes were interred in the Kirkyard of Alford. There are memorial gates at Murray Park, Alford, officially opened in 1956. The Charles Murray Memorial Trust, founded in 1942, arranged publication of his **Last Poems** in 1969 and **Hamewith - the complete poems of Charles Murray** in 1979.

A bust and two portraits, one by his daughter Sheila, are in Aberdeen Art Gallery.

John A. L. Gilfillan

Carolina Oliphant

Carolina Oliphant, Lady Nairne

Poet

Carolina Oliphant was born at Gask, Perthshire, on 16th August 1766. The Oliphants of Gask and her mother's family, the Robertsons of Struan, were noted for their unswerving loyalty to the Jacobite cause. Both Carolina's father and grandfather were "out" in the '45 Rising and had to leave Scotland after Culloden. The family home was secured by relatives buying it in the sale of forfeited estates.

This family sympathy for the Jacobite cause is reflected in much of Oliphant's work, such as **The Hundred Pipers, Will ye no Come back again** and **Wha'll be King but Charlie?** Her own sympathies were, however, much wider and in **The Pentland Hills,** a poem on the Covenanters - men and women who, she wrote, had:

> *...so much right feeling and heroism amongst them that they merit a place in Scottish song*

she even criticised the great Jacobite hero figure James Graham of Claverhouse:

> *Oh, Claverhouse! fell Claverhouse!*
> *Thou brave but cruel Graham!*
> *Dark deeds like thine will last for aye,*
> *Linked wi' thy blighted name.*

Oliphant's feeling for landscape and nature is reflected in works like **The Auld House** (a tribute to her birthplace, the Old House of Gask) and **The Rowan Tree** and her appreciation of the human comedy is shown in **The Laird o' Cockpen.** A more serious note was struck in poems like **Caller Herring:**

> *Wha'll buy my caller herrin'?*
> *Oh, ye may call them vulgar farin' -*
> *Wives and mithers, maist desparin',*
> *Ca' them lives o' men.*

and in the moving **The Land o' the Leal,** a poem inspired by the death of a friend's infant daughter.

Much of her work was published anonymously - contemporary convention frowning on a woman in her social position writing for publication. She was a keen collector of folk tunes, providing new words for those that inspired her - as did her contemporaries, Burns and Hogg. Much of her work was contributed in this form, under the pen-name of Mrs Bogan of Bogan, to Robert Purdie's **The Scottish Minstrel** (1821-24) edited by R. A. Smith.

In 1806 aged 41, she married her second cousin, Major William Nairne. They had one son, born in 1808. In 1824, following George IV's visit to Edinburgh in 1822 and Walter Scott's campaigning, Parliament restored the forfeited Jacobite peerages and Major Nairne regained the family Barony. He died in 1830 and Lady Nairne later travelled in Europe with her invalid son who died in 1837. She died at Gask, aged 79, on 26th October 1845 and a posthumous collection of verse, **Lays of Strathearn,** was prepared by her sister. A granite cross was erected to her memory in the grounds of Gask House.

A collection of sixteen **Songs by Lady Nairne** was published by Akros in 1996 and a number of her songs and poems are widely anthologised.

Brian D. Osborne

Margaret Oliphant

Novelist

Margaret Oliphant

Margaret Oliphant, 1828-1897, an extremely prolific writer, produced several novels and stories that place her in the front rank of Victorian fiction. Born at Wallyford, East Lothian, she grew up mainly in Glasgow and Liverpool. She was an avid reader and began to write at an early age, publishing her first novel, **Passages in the Life of Margaret Maitland,** in 1849. Thereafter, for the best part of half a century, she produced fiction, biography, travel books and articles on a vast range of topics.

Although she lived only for short periods in Scotland, many of her novels have Scottish themes, both historical and contemporaneous. Among her earlier Scottish novels is **Katie Stewart, a true story** (1853), set in 1745 and drawing on her own family background. A later Scottish novel, **Effie Ogilvie** (1886), explores the difficulties of a young woman longing to be more than a merely decorative wife.

After the death of her husband in 1859, Oliphant relied on her writing to support her family. She had to take on journalistic work and wrote frequently for **Blackwood's Magazine.** She felt that the pressure to write for money denied her the opportunity to produce first-rate work, but nevertheless she had a "powerful impulse towards excellence", a phrase she uses of one of her own characters, which led to some impressive fiction. After decades of neglect, her achievement is now beginning to be recognised.

The first fiction to become popular was the group of novels known as **The Carlingford Chronicles**, closely-observed and vividly comic narratives of domestic and clerical life. Most telling of these is **Miss Marjoribanks** (1866) in which spirited and gently satiric characterisation produces a substantial and highly entertaining novel. Her later novels tend to be darker in tone, anti-romantic and critical of entrenched social values.

Much of her fiction examines the position of women and the injustice and sterility of denying women outlets of fulfilment. **Hester** (1883) addresses this issue uncompromisingly, as does **Kirsteen** (1890), one of her last and best novels. She tackled marital unhappiness and the relations between parents and children with a relentlessly realistic intelligence. **The Ladies Lindores** (1883) and **A Country Gentleman and his Family** (1886) are powerful examples.

Oliphant's stories of the supernatural are among her best work, psychologically perceptive and with lasting resonance: **The Library Window** is one of the most subtly modulated Scottish short stories ever to be written. Although her work often shows the strain of being turned out under pressure, Margaret Oliphant was an acutely observant and formidably intelligent novelist. Her trenchant voice, narrative drive and ironic exposure of injustice and hypocrisy provide an invaluable commentary on Victorian society. Her prose is purposeful rather than elegant, with a rugged integrity and often subversive in both intention and result.

Useful introductions to Oliphant's work include **The Autobiography of Margaret Oliphant** (edited Elisabeth Jay), 1990; **Margaret Oliphant: A Critical Biography** by Merryn Williams, 1986 and **Margaret Oliphant** by Jenni Calder 1996.

Jenni Calder

Allan Ramsay

Poet

Allan Ramsay

Allan Ramsay was born in the remote Lanarkshire village of Leadhills in 1685. Around 1704 he moved to Edinburgh and became an apprentice wigmaker. Completing his apprenticeship in 1709, Ramsay became a Burgess the following year and opened a shop in the Grassmarket.

During this period Scotland was in a sad state of decline. Politically weakened by the Act of Union (1707) she was also in danger of cultural domination by England. Ramsay, a strong nationalist, became increasingly involved in Edinburgh intellectual and literary circles from 1710 on. In 1712 he co-founded the Easy Club a society with strong Jacobite leanings which met to discuss literature and politics. Many of Ramsay's early poems received their first public airing when read aloud to club members. Although sympathetic to the cause, Ramsay had no involvement in either the 1715 or 1745 Jacobite uprisings.

By 1720 Ramsay's interest in literature was such that he abandoned wigmaking and became a bookseller. In 1725 he moved to premises in the High Street where he opened what is generally regarded as Britain's first circulating library.

By this time he had become a successful poet, publishing his first collection of verse in 1721 and second in 1728. Ramsay wrote in both Scots and English but with markedly more success in the former. His "English" poems owe too obvious a debt to Alexander Pope, whereas his verse in Scots did much to initiate the eighteenth century revival of Scottish vernacular poetry - later continued by Fergusson and Burns.

Ramsay also deserves credit for his rediscovery of an earlier Scottish tradition. As the editor of **The Evergreen** (1724) he anthologised the work of long neglected poets including Dunbar and Henryson. **The Tea Table Miscellany** (5 volumes 1724-37) resurrected many traditional songs and ballads. He has, with some justice, been criticised for bowdlerising and altering the texts of these poems and songs but he performed a vital service in rescuing Scotland's forgotten literary legacy.

In 1736 Ramsay opened the New Theatre in Carruber's Close. Unfortunately, it soon fell foul of the 1737 Licensing Act and was closed, losing him a lot of money. Thereafter he retired to his house on the Castlehill until his death in 1758.

Ramsay frequently spent time at the home of his friends the Forbes of Newhall. Newhall House has been identified as the setting of his greatest triumph, the pastoral comedy **The Gentle Shepherd** (1725). It concerns rustic life and courtship amongst the Pentland Hills. A huge popular success, it also received extravagant praise from, amongst others, Fergusson, Burns and James Boswell who spoke of its "real picture of manners" and "beautiful rural imagery":

> *Gae far'er up the burn to Habbie's How,*
> *Where a' the sweets o' spring and summer grow:*
> *There 'tween twa birks, out ower a little lin,*
> *The water fa's and maks a singin' din;*
> *A pool breast-deep, beneath as clear as glass,*
> *Kisses, wi' easy whirls, the bord'ring grass.*

Sandy Winton

Alexander Scott

Poet

Scott's date of birth is uncertain, but was probably around 1515. Little is known of his early life and career. From his work, however, it is evident that he was familiar with Dalkeith and Edinburgh, and his friendship with Alexander Montgomerie and other courtiers indicates residence in the capital.

Scott was presented to the prebend of the Chapel Royal, Stirling in 1539 and in 1548 he became musician and organist at Inchmahome Priory. Following the death of the Priory's commendator, Robert Erskine, at the Battle of Pinkie, 1547, he composed **Lament of the Master of Erskine**.

Through his connections with the Erskine family Scott visited France and came into contact with the court of Mary, Queen of Scots, there. His concern with the political and religious issues of the time are revealed in **Ane New Year Gift to the Queen Mary, when she come first hame, 1562**. The poem is an even-handed appeal to the young Queen, denouncing the corrupt ways of the Catholic Church and warning against the "cuvatyce of geir" among Reformers. By 1565 Scott was a canon at Inchaffray in Perthshire and in 1567 he purchased Nether Petledie estate in Fife and became a wealthy landowner.

It appears that he was married. To the poem **To Luve Unluvit** was added a footnote that it was written "quhen his wife left him". The accuracy of this is open to doubt. It may have been appended by Scott himself; equally it may be by a scribe who copied the poem into the Bannatyne Manuscript.

All of Scott's thirty six extant poems are to be found in the Bannatyne Manuscript which contains the only contemporary collection of his work. Otherwise, he would be known only by mention in a sonnet by Montgomerie.

In the main, the poems fall into two categories: courtly love lyrics, some of which were composed to dance tunes, and poems describing the spectrum of emotions experienced by those in love.

Scott's namesake and editor of the 1952 collection of his work describes him as:

> ... a weathercock of the emotions, twirling about in the winds of passion and pointing now to praise, now to dispraise, as the mood of the moment directs.

In successfully portraying the contradictions and confusions of love Scott is considered by many to be the finest Scottish love poet before Burns.

Although included among the "makars", he has been compared with the English poet, Sir Thomas Wyatt. **A Rondel of Love** is well-known and has been much anthologised:

> Lo! What it is to love,
> Learn ye, that list to prove,
> Be me, I say, that no ways may
> The grund of grief remove,
> Bot still decay, both nicht and day;
> Lo! What it is to love.

Although uncertain, the date of Alexander Scott's death is usually given as 1583.

Alan Reid

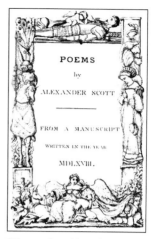

Title page from Alexander Scott's "Poems".

Sir Walter Scott

Novelist & poet

Sir Walter Scott

Walter Scott was born on 15th August 1771 in the Old Town of Edinburgh. Later, the family moved (in a manner very reminiscent of **Redgauntlet**) to the clean air of George Square where Scott grew up, with a brief but vital interlude in the Borders to help the sickly boy — though it did not prevent an attack of polio which gave him a lame leg for life. He grew up full of energy, pursued school and university with enthusiasm but even more enthusiasm went into his reading, collecting Scottish Border ballads (to become **Minstrelsy of the Scottish Border**), learning German (he was an early translator of Schiller and Bürger), and trying his own hand at poetry.

Scott was a man of prodigious energy as well as talent. All his adult life he was a working lawyer, but this did not prevent him from a social life which put him at the centre of literary Edinburgh (some would say, literary Scotland) and a steady involvement in prose writing, reviewing and periodical publication. Nor did it prevent his original writing. As well as ballad collections and translations, his earliest major success was in poetry: **The Lay of the Last Minstrel** (1805), **Marmion** (1808) and — outstandingly — **The Lady of the Lake** (1810). "Hail Caledonia, stern and wild!", wrote Scott, and this was the country of his poems, wild, historical, bloody, romantic, mysterious: the poetry (which was widely translated and imitated) set in people's minds an idea of Scotland still hard to dislodge.

No one thing would ever satisfy Scott, however. He took to castle-building — his gothic pile of Abbotsford near Melrose — and to entertaining, and he saw the threat that Byron posed to his supremacy as poet. The answer was **Waverley** (1814), a *tour de force* which catapulted historical fiction into public consciousness and popularity, and made Scott world famous again, this time as the anonymous (though it was an open secret) "Author of Waverley" . A stream of successes followed, including **Guy Mannering** (1815), **The Antiquary** (1816), **Old Mortality** (1816). **Rob Roy** (1818), **The Heart of Midlothian** (1818) and — best of all — **Redgauntlet** (1824).

The dates tell their own story. This is a massive output of multi-volume novels by a hard-working public figure who travelled and entertained on a grand scale. Slowly the truth has emerged of how Scott would write at unbelievable speed — early mornings, often — and the result would be painstakingly transcribed for him, made legible and punctuated, the little slips caught and generally tidied up before the result — in a new handwriting, of course, to preserve the author's thin anonymity — went to the publisher. But the process was exhausting: so was the pace of Scott's life, and his appetite for money, which led him to the serious mistake of quietly buying a stake in both his printer and his publisher.

While things went well, he reaped a handsome reward: when both went down in the financial crash of 1826, Scott was cruelly exposed and bankrupted on a massive scale. The story of his response to ruin (nobly faced up to in his very readable **Journal**) is well known: he buckled to, and simply worked harder than ever for the six remaining years of his life. He produced a torrent of work, fiction and critical prose mostly, which slowly but steadily paid off his patient creditors, but at a terrible price to Scott's health. A series of strokes crippled him, and he died in 1832 — though the sale of his copyrights pretty well paid off his debts. Despite all, these late years produced wonderful work of the quality of **The Chronicles of the Canongate,** which included **The Fair Maid of Perth** (1828).

The story of Scott's life is little more incredible than his fiction. Yet despite the huge success of his poetry, and the real solid values of his massive output in critical and controversial prose and biography, it is the fiction which is the basis of his enduring reputation. In the historical work he ranges far from a Scotland he knew intimately (though a rather sketchier Gaelic Scotland which he approached more timidly) to England, Europe, the East: in time he ranges from the mediaeval to the very recent.

A central, and very successful, strategy is to create a "Scott hero", and make him (it is usually him) experience events which are largely verifiable history, indeed meet real historical characters, while the central "Scott hero" remains pure fiction. Since the hero is often an outsider, it is necessary to explain everything to him, scenery, history, speech: in this way the outsider/reader can understand too and have battle scenes (like Prestonpans in **Waverley**) or domestic detail (like Edinburgh's New Town in **Redgauntlet**) or historical personages (like Argyle in **The Heart of Midlothian**) explained without holding up the flow of the narrative.

Scott excels in fast-paced battle scenes, sweeping scene setting (Edinburgh at the start of **The Antiquary,** Glasgow in **Rob Roy**) and interesting travel. He is slower in domestic settings and some of his female characters (Rose and Flora in **Waverley,** to name but two) can be wooden and mechanical. His working-class characters are often easier and lighter: Jeanie Deans in **The Heart of Midlothian** is an outstanding case, and like many of Scott's working-class characters she speaks an easy and unembarrassed Scots which is one of the great contributions he made to the history of the Scottish novel.

Scott's influence is not just on fiction: painting and opera are only two of the creative arts where his scenes and characters are much reproduced, and the whole picture of what Scotland is, and was, came to be heavily derived from Scott's work. His poetry is sadly neglected today: his novels, lengthy and often slow-moving at the outset are only now regaining their popular esteem. But publication of a proper modern edition (incredibly, the first) of his fiction is ensuring a steady renewal of his stature as a writer of the world class.

Ian Campbell

The Scott Monument, Princes Street, Edinburgh

William Sharp

Novelist

William Sharp

Son of a muslin manufacturer and a mother with Scandinavian blood, William Sharp was born in Paisley on 12th September 1855 and left when aged 12 years. "Celt in heart and spirit" he was a delicate "merry and mischievous" child, also a loner with a strong imagination. From his Highland nurse, and reinforced in later life by many visits there, he learned about the Celtic sagas. He attended Glasgow University but did not graduate. Diligent but unconventional, his interests included nature, folklore and foreign languages and literature.

He found work with a lawyer, but an attack of typhoid so weakened him that he went to Australia to recuperate. Based on this visit was his first novel **Sport of Chance** (1888).

Returned from Australia, he worked for a bank in London and on medical advice turned down the offer of a literary professorship. While in London, his move into a career in writing was influenced by the artist, Sir Joseph Noel Paton, a one-time pattern designer in Paisley. In 1884 he had married his cousin Elizabeth A. Sharp, editor of **Lyra Celtica**. After the success of **Sonnets of this Century** (1886), Sharp also wrote dramas and biographies of literary figures.

Following a visit to Rome he produced **Sospiri di Roma** (1891), poems in irregular meter. When there he became friendly with a lady whose personality symbolised to him the heroic women of Greek and Celtic days. As "Fiona MacLeod" he dedicated **Pharais** (1894) to her, a story full of "Celtic romance … and the mysterious". In **The Mystic's Prayer** (s)he asks for help:

> *In flame of sunrise bathe my mind*
> *O Master of the Hidden Fire*
> *That, when I wake, clear eyed may be*
> *My soul's desire.*

The Gaelic language, his nurse's tales and his friend in Rome all influenced **Pharais**. This was the first of his versions of the neo-Celtic legends, written as by Fiona MacLeod, whose identity only became known after Sharp's death. The Sharps themselves were childless and looked on "Fiona" as their daughter.

The "continual play of the two forces" - the literary Sharp and the Celtic dreamer MacLeod - at one time brought him near to nervous collapse. He died in Sicily on 12th December 1905 and is remembered by a Celtic Cross cut into the lava of Mount Etna. Regarded as the father figure of the Celtic Renaissance, Sharp's knowledge of Gaelic culture has been criticised. He is commemorated in his home town by a double-image portrait in Paisley's Central Library. Works by and about him, notably a **Memoir** by his wife, can be seen in the Local Studies Collection. Sharp's dichotomy is said to have been bridged in part by "Wilfion", a fusion of his two selves. This name was revived in 1975 when the academic publisher, Wilfion Books, was set up. **The Wilfion Scripts,** published by them in 1980, purports to have been dictated by Sharp through a medium.

Ken Hinshalwood

Nan Shepherd

Novelist, critic & lecturer

Nan Shepherd

Anna (Nan) Shepherd was born on 11th February 1893. Her father, John Shepherd, was an engineer. She was brought up in West Cults, Aberdeenshire and lived there most of her adult life. She attended Aberdeen High School for Girls, proceeding to the University of Aberdeen from which she graduated in 1915. Thereafter she lectured in English Literature at Aberdeen College of Education until her retirement in 1956. She wrote three novels, **The Quarry Wood** (1928), **The Weatherhouse** (1930) and **A Pass in the Grampians** (1933); a volume of poetry **In the Cairngorms** (1934) and a volume of non-fiction **The Living Mountain**, a celebration of the Cairngorms which though not published until 1977, was written in the 1940s. After her retirement she edited the **Aberdeen University Review**. She was awarded an honorary degree by Aberdeen University in 1964. She died in Woodend Hospital, Aberdeen on 23rd February 1981. Nan Shepherd was a great literary encourager. Jessie Kesson benefited from her support. She also corresponded with other literary figures, particularly Neil Gunn who had a similar attitude to the spiritual qualities of landscape. In a letter from 1970 Gunn summed up Shepherd's love of place and her gift for companionship: "I came across some of your old letters. Marvellous …You're like a lovely day on the hills."

Nan Shepherd's work is an outstanding contribution to the Modernist fiction of Scotland. **The Quarry Wood** published four years before Lewis Grassic Gibbon's **Sunset Song**, shares the same setting in a small North-East community. However, instead of Gibbon's elegy for a past way of life and the unique style in which he conveys it, Shepherd's fiction, is less pessimistic about the future seeing in the goal of a university education for Martha, the ploughman's daughter, a route to personal freedom. Sadness in Shepherd's fiction is for the restricted lives of women. Martha takes it for granted that she should look after her Aunt Josephine in her last illness although Martha has a full-time job. In **The Weatherhouse**, Mrs Falconer has never been able to leave her imagination and live in reality at all. She comes to realise this when she is old and her last years are tormented by what she has lost and clumsy attempts to live more authentically. She loses her faith and dies murmuring incoherently about her life. Shepherd is fiercely realistic in depicting the depredations of a confined life, illness and death and their consequences for those who care for the sick. Much of this realism comes from Shepherd's ability to describe and analyse complex emotions. Martha's tragedy is that she falls in love with a married man. Shepherd is able to convey the emotions of love, guilt, desire, and loss in their interminable wranglings in the inner self when the outer self seems composed with a depth of penetration which is reminiscent of D.H. Lawrence. Shepherd, however, does not solve Martha's loneliness by marriage but through her fostering a little illegitimate boy. Women's capacity to find satisfying emotional fulfilment in relationships other than heterosexual union is also attested by writers as diverse as Jane and Helen Findlater, Willa Muir and Anna Buchan.

Beth Dickson

Photo: Gordon Wright

Sydney Goodsir Smith

Sydney Goodsir Smith

Poet, playwright & critic

Born in Wellington, New Zealand on 25th October 1915, Sydney Goodsir Smith's father was an army medical officer, and his mother was Scottish. He was educated in England at Malvern College before starting a medical degree at Edinburgh University, where his father was professor of forensic medicine. Hating anatomy, he abandoned this degree and went to Oxford instead to study at Oriel College. Thereafter he returned to Scotland, whose culture and history he enthusiastically embraced, and which was to form the basis of all his subsequent work.

Now viewed by some as an equal with Hugh MacDiarmid as a poet of the Scottish Renaissance, Goodsir Smith quickly adopted Scots for his poetry, appropriating many archaicisms and delving deep into the late medieval tradition of Scottish makars for stylistic inspiration. Although plainly influenced by poets such as Dunbar and Henryson and Gawain Douglas, he fused his admiration for their technique with his own very distinctive, sometimes unwieldy language, creating a vibrant, romantic and frequently bawdy voice.

His first collection, **Skail Wind**, was published in 1941, but it was not until his third collection, **The Deevil's Waltz** (1946), that he showed the extent of his talent. A poet with a Rabelaisian enjoyment of words and literary texture, he at times strained the reader's - or performer's - patience, as with his hilarious novel, **Carotid Cornucopius** (1947), in which he draws a vivid picture of Edinburgh low life, replete with wit, vulgarity, affection and such detonations as:

> *...whaile owre the sceane rained hiech in the havens the gloarianguished dumble-watergaw in ilka calour in the spookitrain, frae gowden yellow til the dowpest impurpietrude...*

Goodsir Smith's play, **The Wallace**, performed at the Edinburgh Festival of 1960, was not wholly a success, striving to cover too much ground in an idiom compromised by his attempt to cater for a partly English audience. Nevertheless it showed again the poet's fondness for tongue-twisting vocabulary. Actor Iain Cuthbertson, who played Wallace, commented that the language "was eminently speakable, once one had a firm grip of one's dentures".

Goodsir Smith's finest work was his twenty-four part celebration of romantic love, **Under the Eildon Tree** (1948), described by fellow poet Alexander Scott as "the greatest extended poem on passion in the whole Scots tradition". By turns rumbustious, tender and tragic, it is the best example of his ability to combine a wide range of emotions and tone, of his talent at evoking atmosphere, at poking fun at himself, and at creating a realistically fragmented sliver of human experience.

Goodsir Smith was for several years art critic for **The Scotsman**. He was a dedicated amateur painter, a gifted translator of such writers as Tristan Corbière and Alexander Blok, and was widely loved for his wit, intelligence and good humour. Although his literary output was relatively small, it achieved considerable recognition, both for himself and for the richness and versatility of the Scots language. He died in 1975. What survives in print is only an echo of the man in person.

Rosemary Goring

Tobias George Smollett

Novelist

Tobias Smollett

Smollett was a less prolific novelist than Scott, and his books are not as readable as Stevenson's, but he was the first Scottish novelist and he has never been surpassed. Indeed, Smollett can be said to have prefigured the Scottish fiction of the nineties of the twentieth century - the fiction of Irvine Welsh and his contemporaries, descriptive of low life as it really is. It is unlikely that critics nowadays would malign an author for satire which made readers writhe, or for the grotesqueness of his imagery, but Smollett was upbraided for this, and, even, for his use of researchers in wide-ranging works of non-fiction. Smollett was an original whose worth has rarely been properly acknowledged, not least because his contemporaries, Fielding, Richardson and Sterne, were in the same class as he was, but also because he was an Anglo-Scot whose countrymen have never identified with him in the same way as they identified, for example with the other exile Stevenson.

He was born in 1721 at Dalquhurn in Renton, Dumbartonshire, and educated at the University of Glasgow. His early life is strongly hinted at in his first successful comic novel, **Roderick Random** (1748); both his learned schoolmaster in Dumbarton, and his first employer in Glasgow are satirised in it. At fourteen he was apprenticed to a Glasgow doctor, and lived in a back attic in Gibson's Land in the merchant city of the Glasgow tobacco barons.

He became a surgeon's mate in the navy and, later, in 1744, began practice as a surgeon in the London of Johnson, Garrick and Handel. His first literary work was an historical play called **The Regicide** about James I which he conceived in Glasgow. It was refused by Garrick, who was never quite forgiven, and others.

He then turned to political satire, but it was his picaresque novels that made him famous. **Roderick Random** is a vigorous, coarse comedy about sailors' lives during the British expedition against Cartagena in the West Indies in the War of Jenkins' Ear of 1739-41 (one of the most farcical episodes in British history). It places Smollett in the first rank as a novelist of the sea. He met and married his beloved wife in the West Indies, and encountered Robert Graham of Gartmore, a lifelong friend, there. The expedition to Cartagena later landed him in gaol for libel, when Admiral Knowles published a pamphlet defending his competence in a disastrous raid on Rochefort, and Smollett drew attention to his defects in one of the finest pieces of sustained invective in the English language.

Smollett was his own worst enemy and succeeded in offending many people. Never quite well, he had a short temper and was free with plain insults, and, worse, bitter irony. He quarrelled with Rich, the manager of Covent Garden and, as a consequence, his masque **Alceste** to music by Handel was never performed. The composer is reported as saying "Dat Scot is ein tam fool; I could have made his vork immortal!" However, his friends included Dr Alexander Carlyle and Dr John Moore, his first biographer, both of whom found much to delight them in the irascible author.

Several other episodic novels, full of grotesque characters and broad satire, among them **The Adventures of Peregrine Pickle** (1751), a well-regarded satire on the Grand Tour, and **Ferdinand Count Fathom** (1753) came next, and were so successful that Smollett abandoned his practice of surgery. As a Doctor he was a great advocate of spas and one of the first to promote sea bathing. Indeed, he was an early tourist, and it is a matter for great regret that he did not write up his occasional visits to Scotland because what is often regarded as his finest work is **Travels in France and Italy** (1766), a witty and perceptive journal of a tour in search of good health late in life.

However, his last novel, **The Expedition of Humphry Clinker** (1771), written in Italy during the last two years of his life, told in a series of letters, is about the travels of a family through England and Scotland and deals with sex, politics and religion in resorts for gentlefolk. The Scottish passages are probably based on his long visit in 1766 when he saw his sister in Edinburgh, and his old friends in Edinburgh and Glasgow. They are particularly funny and display his real affection for his native land. There is a shrewd portrait, too, of "Doctor Smollett" in Chelsea, surrounded by minor authors and hangers-on.

Smollett's comic inventiveness influenced Sheridan, Dickens and Thackeray, and Scott paid tribute to his impact on him, pointing out Smollett's ability to make readers laugh out loud. Smollett's other books include a **Complete History of England** (1757-58), which was popular and financially successful, **The Present State of All Nations,** a world geography, notable for its time, and **The History and Adventures of an Atom** (1769), a coarse satire on English public affairs.

Smollett played a part in Britain's first Scottish administration, that of the Earl of Bute. After editing the **Critical Review** (1756-63), he produced **The Briton** (1762-63) a government propaganda sheet, which more than met its match in the opposition's **North Briton**, edited by Wilkes. He also translated the French picaresque romance **Gil Blas** by Le Sage and the Spanish classic **Don Quixote.** His poetry includes **The Tears of Scotland**, a heartfelt lament for Culloden, and his **Ode to Leven Water**, celebrating the famous river which flowed past his childhood home.

Smollett died an invalid near Leghorn in Italy in 1771. His monument in Renton, a fine Tuscan column with a Latin inscription partly by Johnson, is worth visiting as it is the focal point of a number of sites associated with him described mainly in **Humphry Clinker**. His sister's house at the head of St John Street in Edinburgh has a plaque. **Smollett's Scotland** by Louis Stott deals with these and other localities. The most recent biography is Louis Knapp's **Tobias Smollett** (1949). Smollett's principal novels are readily available in paperback.

Louis Stott

William Soutar

Poet

William Soutar was born in Perth on 28th April 1898. A pupil at Perth Academy in 1916, he went straight into the Navy. On demobilization he entered Edinburgh University, and before graduating in 1923 he had published his first book of poems. An illness contracted during his service, "a form of spondylitis", crippled him increasingly, and after an unsuccessful operation in 1930 he was confined to bed for more than thirteen years until his death on 15th October 1943.

Soutar wrote poetry both in English and in Scots. His earlier English poems are sensitive, but now seem a little faded. With the coming of war the urgency of his pacifism brought a vision, and the skill to express it in powerful poems such as **The Children** and **The Permanence of the Young Men**.

As early as 1923, inspired and encouraged by Hugh MacDiarmid, Soutar had begun to write poems in Scots, and he was further stimulated in this direction by the arrival in 1927, shortly before her sixth birthday, of his parents' adopted daughter, Evelyn, a distant relative who had been orphaned in Australia. Soutar became the little girl's companion, both at work and at play, as his diaries reveal. A happy result was the book, appropriately dedicated "To Evelyn", **Seeds in the Wind: poems in Scots for children** (1933).

His bairn-rhymes and riddles are a seminal part of his work, but Soutar's most original contribution to the Scottish literary tradition is the series of poems he called "whigmaleeries". These are usually short, written in a colloquial idiom, comic in the widest definition of that word, surveying the human comedy with kindly interest and a shrewd perception of the incongruities of life. They puncture pomposity through their skilful use of what Soutar called the *aff-takin* power of Scots. MacDiarmid recognized the poet's "rare and important achievement: a comic poetry - at once really comic and really poetry".

Soutar published ten slim volumes of poetry, and an eleventh, **The Expectant Silence**, which he had prepared for the press, appeared in 1944. His **Collected Poems**, edited by MacDiarmid, was published in 1948, but the title is erroneous; the volume omits all the poems printed in the previously published collections and a considerable number from the poet's diaries and notebooks. The "new selection" of his poems, published in 1988, draws on the totality of his verse.

But Soutar was more than a poet. In the Soutar archive in the National Library the prose manuscripts are more extensive than the poetry: his diaries, complete from 1917 to 1943; his journals, kept concurrently with his diaries from 1930 to 1940; and a unique series of thirty-four "Dream Books".

Very little of the prose has been published. Alexander Scott, author of a critical biography of Soutar, **Still Life**, edited a selection published as **Diaries of a Dying Man** in 1954 (reissued in paperback in 1991), but a further more generous selection is required to reveal, in Duncan Glen's words, "a body of work worthy to be beside his poetry".

W. R. Aitken

William Soutar

R.L. Stevenson

Robert Louis Stevenson

Poet, novelist & essayist

Robert Louis Stevenson was at the height of his powers when he died suddenly in Samoa in 1894. For a long period he was thought of mainly as the writer of adventure stories for children, but now there is growing recognition of his subtle and surprisingly modern explorations of dilemmas of character and action.

Stevenson grew up in Edinburgh, and this profoundly shaped his writing. He was born on 13th November 1850 and from earliest childhood he was frequently ill, which influenced a fertile imagination. It was assumed that Stevenson would follow the profession of his father, Thomas Stevenson, a distinguished lighthouse and harbour engineer, and he studied engineering at Edinburgh University. However, in his twenty-first year he announced his intention of becoming a writer.

He began with essays and travel writing and within a few years was recognised as a writer of great promise. His first commercially published book, **An Inland Voyage**, (1878) described a canoe trip in Belgium and France. He followed this in 1879 with **Edinburgh, Picturesque Notes** and an account of a walking tour in the Cevennes, **Travels with a Donkey**. Although he began writing fiction as a teenager, it was not until 1877 that his first short story was published, and 1882 before he began to publish longer fiction. **Treasure Island**, serialised in that year, was published in volume form in 1883. He did not become popular until 1886, with the publication of **Kidnapped** and **Strange Case of Dr Jekyll and Mr Hyde**, the first gaining critical esteem, the second a best-seller which made his reputation on both sides of the Atlantic.

Stevenson was absorbed by Scottish history and Scottish character, and this fascination is an essential aspect of his writing. He also examined, in **Jekyll and Hyde** and elsewhere, what he considered to be the hypocrisy of Victorian values. His own bohemianism flouted convention, and his marriage to Fanny Osbourne, an American divorcee ten years his senior, caused some distress to friends and family.

From his early twenties, ill-health kept him away from Scotland for long periods. But he continued to write about Scotland, and some of his most powerful short stories, **Thrawn Janet** and **The Merry Men** for example, have Scottish themes. In these stories, as well as in **Kidnapped** and later fiction such as **The Master of Ballantrae** (1888), he examined some of the extreme and contrary currents of Scotland's past, often projecting a dualism of both personality and belief. This dualism is most famous in **Jekyll and Hyde** and **Kidnapped**, whose two central characters are David Balfour, a Lowland Whig, and Alan Breck Stewart, a Highland Jacobite. The novel revolves around their friendship and their differences, suggesting a metaphor for Scotland itself.

Stevenson lived for several years in Switzerland, France and the south of England. In 1887, after the death of his father, he went to America. From there he continued west, embarking on a voyage through the South Pacific, accompanied by Fanny and his widowed mother. He wrote about his Pacific voyages in numerous articles which were published in volume form as **In the South Seas** (1892). He never returned to Scotland. He had at last found a climate that suited his health, and decided to settle on the island of Upolu in

Samoa. It was there in his house Vailima that he spent the last years of his life.

The South Pacific opened new subjects for his writing. He responded to island culture with sympathetic understanding, comparing the erosion of traditions to the experience of Highland culture in Scotland. He was critical of the exploitative impact of Europeans and Americans, and in Samoa adopted the cause of a Polynesian chief who was defeated in a brief episode of civil war. He described this in **A Footnote to History** (1892). His South Sea experiences also produced fiction, and for almost the first time he turned his attention to the contemporary scene. He drew directly on Polynesian tradition to write **The Bottle Imp** and **The Isle of Voices** and the epic poem **Rahero**, but his story **The Beach of Falesa** is rather different. It explores the clash of cultures between white traders and islanders and is one of Stevenson's best pieces of fiction. His novel **The Ebb Tide** (1894) is a remarkable study of morality and individual responsibility, themes that had absorbed him earlier. The mature stylist, combining precision and complexity, is seen at his most challenging.

Stevenson collaborated with his stepson Lloyd Osbourne to write **The Wrong Box** (1889), a rather heavy-handed comedy, and **The Wrecker** (1892), a Pacific adventure story. The immediacy and creative stimulus of the Pacific was strong, but Scotland continued to inspire both fiction and poetry. It was at Vailima that he wrote **Catriona** (1893), a sequel to **Kidnapped, St Ives** (unfinished and published after his death in 1897) and **Weir of Hermiston** (1896, also unfinished). It was **Weir** he was working at on the day he died. Pivoting on the bitterly fraught relationship between a father and son, the novel employs both Scottish tradition and the Scots language with memorable force.

From "A Child's Garden of Verses'. Illustrated by Charles Robinson.

In these last years Stevenson wrote vividly about his native land and some of his most effective poems owe much to the pain of absence. As a poet Stevenson tends to be best remembered as the author of **A Child's Garden of Verses** (1885), poems which communicate the fears as well as the pleasures of childhood, but he also wrote lyric, comic and narrative poems in both Scots and English, published in **Underwoods** (1887) and **Ballads** (1890). His **Collected Poems** (1971) were edited by Janet Adam Smith.

Stevenson was one of the greatest letter writers in the English language, and the complete collection is now available in eight volumes, edited by Bradford A. Booth and Ernest Mehew, 1994-5. These are the best possible introduction to Stevenson's life and work. Biographies include **Voyage to Windward** by J. C. Furnas, 1950; **RLS: A Life Study** by Jenni Calder, 1980; and **Dreams of Exile** by Ian Bell, 1994. The pioneering critical work was **Robert Louis Stevenson** by David Daiches, 1947. This has been followed by a slowly growing critical interest in Europe and North America as well as in Scotland.

Jenni Calder

Annie S Swan

Novelist

Annie Shepherd Swan was born in Edinburgh in 1859, one of a large family which broke up on their mother's death and their father's remarriage. In 1883 Swan married a schoolmaster, James Burnett Smith, who, due to lack of money, had given up the idea of a medical career. Swan encouraged him to resume his studies, supporting him through her writing. On his graduation they moved to England, though maintaining a holiday house in Fife.

Swan's early attempts at writing were financially unrewarding, but **Aldersyde** (1883), her first commercially published novel, met with immediate success. Set in a small Border community, it is something of a blueprint for her later novels, with their recurrent themes of sisterly and motherly love, the virtues of a good woman, and a happy resolution of romantic problems.

Annie S Swan

> *She did not shrink from [his] clasp but moved nearer to him, and laid her head upon his breast. The only thought in her heart was a kind of wondering surprise that she had ever doubted him for a moment. It seemed so natural to feel his arms about her and to know she was the one woman in the world for him.*

Though she had sold the copyright of **Aldersyde** for £50, Swan was now assured of a public for future novels, and began a most prolific writing career. Her books were immensely popular, and she reached an even wider readership through serial publication in **The People's Friend,** which she regarded as the mainstay of her writing life. She was a regular contributor also to other periodicals. She claimed not to know how many books she had written, but bibliographies list over 150.

Reviewing **Carlowrie** (1884), Mrs Oliphant complains that Swan's novels presented an entirely distorted view of Scottish life. Swan protests in reply that she wrote almost entirely of the life she knew. Her later novels hardly support this claim, since she lived a busy and in some ways unconventional life - writing, speaking and travelling - while continuing to produce the wish-fulfilment stories which her readers craved. In her autobiography **My Life** (1934), and her **Letters,** collected in 1945, she appears shrewd, energetic and humorous, but she deplored "the complete overthrow of dignity and reticence" in modern fiction.

Departures from her usual style were stories for the **British Weekly** under the pseudonym "David Lyall". Some of these, dealing with the Boer War, were thought at the time to have been written by a male war correspondent. Her most realistic novel, **The Pendulum** (1926), introduces problems of post-World War I society: a husband admits infidelity, his wife considers divorce, and their daughter spends a weekend with her lover. Though it was published as by "Mrs Burnett Smith", her usual readers identified Swan as the author and were appalled. She did not repeat the experiment.

After her husband's death in 1927 Swan returned to Scotland, where she died at Gullane on 17th June 1943. She is seldom recognised by literary historians, but Charlotte Reid's article **A Cursory Visit of Inspection to Annie S. Swan (Cencrastus,** Winter 1990/91), looks at her life and work, suggesting that a study of her reading public might be of interest.

Moira Burgess

Robert Tannahill

Poet

Robert Tannahill

In 1756 James Tannahill left Kilmarnock for Paisley to find work in the textile trade. He met Janet Pollock of Lochwinnoch, and the couple were married there in 1763. Their son Robert Tannahill, the fifth of eight children, was born on 3rd June 1774 at Castle Street, Paisley. His education consisted of rudimentary reading, writing and accounting at what was called an "English" school. He taught himself the German flute and read widely, having had a talent for verse from an early age. Later, he would develop an interest in theatre, going regularly to performances in Glasgow.

In his twelfth year he was apprenticed to his father (Robert was a weaver all his life). The family had earlier moved to the cottage in Queen Street which was to remain Tannahill's home, except for two years in Bolton between 1800 and 1802. Soon after returning from Bolton his father died and in the eight years following most of his published work was written.

He composed new lyrics to existing airs and had a love of Irish music. R. A. Smith of Paisley and John Ross of Aberdeen set original music to Tannahill's songs. With his work growing in popularity, **The Soldiers Return, A Scottish Interlude in Two Acts, with other poems and songs**, was published in 1807.

Much of his writing was inspired by the countryside surrounding Paisley, where the poet took regular walks, despite a deformity of the right leg. Songs such as **The Braes O' Gleniffer** and **The Flower O' Levern Side** refer to local landmarks and poems like **Will MacNeil's Elegy** and **Allan's Ale** feature local people.

Overall, his work is broad in its understanding of humanity. Descriptions of friendship, love and the responsibility one human being has for another, come up frequently; with the characters being sweethearts, acquaintances and soldiers, lucky or unlucky in love. That he often wrote about soldiers was perhaps due to the impact of recruitment to Scottish Militia Regiments on his everyday life. In June 1809 he wrote to his friend James King, "I see no end of this war system".

> *The Queensferry boatie rows light,*
> *And light is the heart that it bears,*
> *For it brings the poor soldier safe back to his home,*
> *From many long toilsome years.*
> *But fled are his visions of bliss,*
> *All his transports but 'rose to deceive,*
> *For he found the dear cottage a tenantless waste,*
> *And his kindred all sunk in the grave.*
>
> **The Worn Soldier**

Tannahill was prone to bouts of melancholy. His 1810 manuscript was rejected by an Edinburgh publisher, and distressed he "consigned to the flames" as many of his writings as he could. His body was found in a side-tunnel of the Candren Burn, near his home, on 17th May 1810.

That the Paisley Tannahill Club still meets in the Queen Street cottage is a testament to the endurance of his work.

Jim Ferguson

James Thomson

Dramatist & poet

James Thomson

James Thomson was one of the most influential British poets, yet there is no significant writer, before or since, more disparaged. John Veitch in **The Feeling for Nature in Scottish Poetry** offered an explanation for this paradox by pointing out that English was not his native language, but a foreign language which he had to acquire. Thomson's seminal work, **The Seasons** (1726-30, revised 1744), is a laboured and uneasy epic poem, yet it is considered to be the first substantial poem in English to have Nature, or, perhaps, the landscape, as its main subject. Thomson is, properly, credited by historians of the Picturesque, with occupying a position analogous to that of Claude or Poussin in painting. **The Seasons** is said to have inspired Turner, and Wordsworth and Coleridge. Haydn used a translation of **The Seasons** as text for his oratorio **Die Jahreszeiten.**

Thomson was probably born in Ednam, Roxburghshire in 1700, the son of a minister, but he was taken as a babe in arms to the parish of Southdean in a remote fold in the wild hill country under Carter Bar where he was brought up, and of which he may well have been thinking when he celebrated:

> *Rough rugged rocks, wet marshes, ruined towers,*
> *Bare trees, brown brakes, bleak heaths, and rushy moors*

He was educated - reluctantly it is said - at the University of Edinburgh. He published poetry there, but left university early and made his way to London. Thomson was best known in his own lifetime as a dramatist.

Although **The Seasons** was written in London, it undoubtedly owes much to his boyhood:

> *…in my cheerful morn of life,*
> *When nursed by careless solitude I lived,*
> *And sung of Nature with unceasing joy,*
> *Pleased have I wandered through your rough domain;*

Other influences from Scotland occur in **The Seasons.** There are significant echoes of Gavin Douglas, of Robert Henryson and, in the following passage, of Alexander Hume:

> *…Gradual sinks the breeze*
> *Into a perfect calm, that not a breath*
> *Is heard to quiver through the closing woods*
> *Or rustling turn the many-twinkling leaves*
> *Of aspen tall…*

Most authorities regard **The Castle of Indolence** (1748) as his finest work; it consists of cantos in Spenserian verse about the pleasures and pitfalls of idleness in which Thomson was something of an expert, eventually occupying a sinecure, rather than having to rely on real work. In 1748, he died in Richmond and is buried there. Among his other writings are the poem **Liberty** (1734-36), and a number of plays. The masque **Alfred** (1740), written with Mallet, contains Arne's famous song **Rule Britannia**. Thomson probably wrote the lyrics. It is for this reason that he is commemorated by a tall, rather unsightly, obelisk in Ednam.

Louis Stott

James Thomson ("B.V.")

Poet

James Thomson

James Thomson was born in Port Glasgow on 23rd November 1834. His father, in the merchant navy, suffered a stroke aboard ship, which caused a character change, making him incapable and depressed. His mother died when he was still a child, leading to his being educated in the Royal Caledonian Orphan Asylum in London and he went on to study to become an army schoolmaster. Although generally competent, he concentrated his attentions on literature, especially Shelley, and translating foreign works.

While training at Ballincollig in Ireland in the early 1850s, he fell deeply in love with a colleague's daughter, Matilda Weller. When about two years later (now at Chelsea) he learned of her death he took it very badly and never fully recovered. His literary works, although often "strikingly original", gave vent to the already present melancholy side of his life. He was to be criticised as an "emotional paralytic" with life (in his own words) "a long defeat".

Perhaps this was in part because he felt unrecognised. His output only appeared in such publications as **Tait's Edinburgh Magazine** and the **National Reformer**, a newspaper owned and edited by a friend, Charles Bradlaugh, and so did not reach a wide readership. The latter pieces were written under the pseudonym "B.V." standing for "Bysshe Vanolis", and showing his love for Percy Bysshe Shelley and the German poet "Novalis" or Hardenberg. **The Doom of a City** written in 1857, though then not published, is said to have exhibited his future "speculative tendency".

Possibly from drink problems, Thomson was discharged from the army in 1862 and helped by Bradlaugh, found a job in a law office. He still wrote but except for the poem **Sunday up the River** had little success.

1872 saw him as a mining agent in the U.S.A., but the mine failed and Bradlaugh now got him a job reporting the war in Spain. His experiences appear in **The Secularist** but as little newsworthy was happening, he was soon recalled, and so ended his series of varied employment.

From then on, Thomson had a meagre existence, relying solely on his writings, but **The City of Dreadful Night**, printed in instalments in **The National Reformer**, did attract some acclaim in literary circles and has been called his greatest work, and also "a modern book of Job". It was eventually published in its own right in 1880. The *Fin de Siècle* pessimism shows in the first stanza of Part III:

> *Although the lamps burn along the silent streets*
> *Even when moonlight silvers empty squares*
> *The dark holds countless lanes and close retreats...*
> *... The lanes are black as subterranean lairs.*

The recognition, however, came too late. Though he struggled to fight his melancholy and alcoholism, and did have further literary achievements, such as **Essays and Phantasies** (1881), James "B.V." Thomson escaped from life's problems on 3rd June 1882 and was buried in Highgate Cemetery. **A Voice from the Nile** (1884) and **Shelley, a Poem** (1885) were published posthumously.

Ken Hinshalwood

Sir Thomas Urquhart

Sir Thomas Urquhart
Man of letters & translator

Urquhart records that he was born, heir to the estates of Cromarty five years after his father's marriage to Christian Elphinston. This suggests 1611 as the year in which one of the most eccentric and humorous of Scottish writers began his eventful life. At the age of eleven he matriculated at Aberdeen University. His lifelong enthusiasm for books on all sorts of subjects and his continuing love affair with words date from this period. Travel abroad followed - the "European tour" being an established way of rounding off a seventeenth century nobleman's education.

At home, one domestic and one national situation complicated his life. His father handled the estates disastrously, and debt and bitter family disputes ensued. Thomas, knighted by Charles I in 1641, consistently opposed the Commonwealth and was, indeed, imprisoned after the Battle of Worcester in 1651. His eventual release may have been contingent on his staying abroad. Certainly, he moved to Europe, living for some time in the Netherlands. The delightful tale that he died there of a fit of laughter on hearing of the Restoration of Charles II in 1660 may be apocryphal but he did die at that time and it accords with his known character.

Life and literature intertwine quite closely in Urquhart's case. His eccentricity and love of words resulted in a number of works which are witty, but so full of Urquhartian coinages, that they run the danger of becoming linguistically impenetrable. These include his mathematical discourse, **Trissotetras**, first published in 1645 and his proposed universal language **Logopandecteision,** which appeared in 1653.

His major claim to literary fame rests on two works. His **Gargantua and Pantagruel** (1653; 1693) - a racy translation of the first three books of Rabelais' comic masterpiece follows in a long line of creative Scottish translations of European literature. Urquhart intelligently chooses to outdo his source in exuberance and has both the vocabulary and the imagination to achieve that aim. His Romance, **Ekskybalauron** or **The Jewel** (1652), on the other hand is the first - very late - work of imaginative prose composed by a Scot. Ironically, it also betrays a keen parodic awareness of an already established tradition in English prose Romance - the high style of Sidney. Thus, when Urquhart's Scottish hero, the Admirable Crichton, finally makes love to his lady, they do not simply look and touch. Rather:

> *...by vertue of the intermutual unlimitedness of their visotactil sensation... the visuriency of either, by ushering the tacturiency of both, made the attrectation of both consequent to the inspection of either. Here was it that action was pasive and action passive, they both being overcome by either- and each the conquerour.*

This is an extreme change from the serious theological and historical tracts which had defined Scottish prose until Urquhart's appearance. The path he forged, however eccentrically, would be followed by George MacKenzie and Smollett. With Sir Thomas, the Scottish novel is born.

R. D. S. Jack

Maurice Walsh

Novelist

Maurice Walsh (1879-1964) was born in Co. Kerry, Ireland, but - in his own phrase - he became sib to Scotland. Seven of his twenty novels have Scottish settings. At one time he was a best selling author in Britain and Ireland and then went out of fashion.

He joined the British Customs and Excise service at a time when Ireland was still part of the United Kingdom and was posted to different parts of Scotland and England. Scotland made a profound impression on him and locations in Skye, Fort William, Clackmannan and particularly Moray, the Cairngorms and the whisky country around Dufftown feature in his novels. He lived for a time in Forres, Moray, and a commemorative plaque about him has been erected at Dallas Dhu distillery, Forres, where he once worked.

Maurice Walsh befriended another Exciseman turned writer, Neil Gunn, and they tried out plots and ideas on one another. It was he who urged Gunn to turn to serious novel writing.

His name was made with a novel of romance in the Highlands, **The Key Above The Door** (1926), first serialised in **Chambers's Journal**, and which became a best seller. The whimsical language can sometimes grate on modern ears, but the underlying theme of the rewards of peace and serenity in outdoor places touched a chord.

A steady stream of novels poured out and nearly all had the same theme of romantic love and manly fights in outdoor settings in Scotland and Ireland, **While Rivers Run** (1928), **The Small Dark Man** (1929), **The Road To Nowhere** (1934), **The Hill is Mine** (1940), **The Spanish Lady** (1943), **Castle Gillian** (1948), **Trouble In the Glen** (1950). He departed from his normal themes to write what he considered to be his best novel, **And No Quarter** (1937), a sword swinging tale of the seventeenth century Scottish Wars of the Covenant. Another of his novels, **Blackcock's Feather** (1932), the story of a Scottish mercenary soldier in Elizabethan Ireland, was used as a history book in Irish schools. Maurice Walsh also wrote comic stories of a Para Handy kind, mainly suited to Irish audiences and based on a character called Thomasheen James, Man-of-no-Work.

One of his short stories, **The Quiet Man**, was filmed in 1952 and still appears on TV screens as a cult film and stars John Wayne and Maureen O'Hara. It is Hollywood's idea of Ireland and the story is superior to the film. **Trouble In The Glen** was (poorly) filmed in 1954 with Orson Welles, Margaret Lockwood and John Laurie in leading roles.

A bust was unveiled in 1995 at Lisselton, Co. Kerry, a ceremony attended by Scottish literary figures.

It is being increasingly realised that amid the whimsy and light tone of the novels his descriptions of scenery and his emphasis on the need for people to value rural and community living, the importance of "belonging" and cherishing a sense of "place", lift him far above the level of pulp fiction.

Rennie McOwan.

Maurice Walsh memorial bust, Co.Kerry.

John Wilson

John Wilson "Christopher North"

Reviewer & essayist

John Wilson was born in 1785 in Paisley, and received his university education in Glasgow and Oxford before settling in Edinburgh, one of a circle of clever young Tory lawyers which included his close friend and collaborator Lockhart. Wilson was a notable man already in his early years, a massive constitution and flowing blond hair, a formidable athletic prowess and a taste for exhibitionism which made him a public figure even before the success of his early poems (**The Isle of Palms, The Magic Mirror, The City of the Plague,** 1812-16). He had some success, too, with sentimental fiction celebrating the pious virtues of Scottish common folks — **Trials of Margaret Lyndsay** (1823) and **The Foresters** (1825).

What catapulted Wilson into the public consciousness was his connection from 1817 to his death with **Blackwood's Edinburgh Magazine,** the source of his critical reputation and his literary disguise as "Christopher North", author of fearsome (and fearless) slashing reviews and literary jokes, rambling commentaries on people and books of the day disguised as conversations in Ambroses's tavern (the **Noctes Ambrosianae** of **Blackwood's,** most but not all by Wilson) and his share in an astonishingly successful but deeply offensive Biblical parody **The Chaldee Manuscript** which helped make **Blackwood's** for October 1817 a best seller. While the manuscript was withdrawn, and public apology made, the object of the exercise - publicity, a good launch for Wilson's editorship - was achieved. Nothing was sacrosanct.

Wilson's courage took him, too, to more controversial heights still when in 1820 the Chair of Moral Philosophy at Edinburgh University came vacant. Wilson was a Tory, and the Town Council who elected the professor shared his politics. Wilson was woefully under-qualified, and there were superb candidates with the wrong politics - Wilson was given the Chair. Oddly, it was a triumph in a way: Wilson turned out to be a public speaker of rare excellence, and his tenure of the Chair attracted generations of students to the subject. What he said was often thin, often borrowed from other sources; but he was one of literary Edinburgh's lions.

This sums up a lot about Wilson. As the influence of Scott waned (Scott died in 1832), as Lockhart left for London in 1825 (to be followed by Francis Jeffrey, and Thomas Carlyle) Wilson was the lion of a diminished literary circle, where he could dominate through personality and through the columns of **Blackwood's,** but where his shaky qualifications were not questioned, measured against his astonishing output of highly readable journalism, and his public performance as "the professor". He remained a lion all his life, and at his death in 1854 literary Scotland was notably quieter without "Christopher North". But perhaps it is a measure of his times, as well as of the man, that a city which supported figures of the stature of Jeffrey, Lockhart, Hogg and Carlyle should turn to Wilson for its literary lion.

Ian Campbell.

Notes on Contributors

W. R. AITKEN, a librarian and bibliographer, was formerly Reader in Librarianship at Strathclyde University and edited the works of Hugh MacDiarmid and William Soutar. [Hugh MacDiarmid; William Soutar]

Carol ANDERSON is a lecturer in Scottish Literature at the University of Glasgow. She has recently edited Violet Jacob's historical novel "Flemington". [Marion Angus; Helen Cruickshank; Violet Jacob]

Ronald ARMSTRONG is a retired primary head-teacher from Dumbarton. He has written on Neil Munro and on Scottish history and culture. [A. J. Cronin]

Rhona ARTHUR is a Professional Officer with the Scottish Library Association and was previously a school librarian in Lanarkshire & Glasgow. [Kenneth Grahame]

Priscilla BAWCUTT lectures in the Department of English Language & Literature at Liverpool University. Her research interests lie in the area of William Dunbar and the Makars. [John Barbour; Gavin Douglas; William Dunbar; Robert Henryson; David Lindsay]

Moira BURGESS, a former librarian, is a novelist, short story writer and literary historian. Author of "The Glasgow Novel" and "Reading Glasgow". [Catherine Carswell; Jane Duncan; David Lindsay; Ian Maclaren; Annie S. Swan]

Jenni CALDER, Publications Officer with the National Museums of Scotland is a poet and has written extensively on Stevenson. [Margaret Oliphant; Robert Louis Stevenson]

Alistair CAMPBELL is Libraries and Museums Manager with Moray Council and has an active interest in the promotion of Scottish literature. [Jessie Kesson]

Ian CAMPBELL is Professor of Scottish and Victorian Literature at Edinburgh University and his research interests include Galt and Thomas Carlyle. [Thomas Carlyle; Lewis Grassic Gibbon; John Gibson Lockhart; Walter Scott; John Wilson]

Robert CRAIG is the Director of the Scottish Library Association and formerly lectured in Librarianship at the University of Strathclyde. [Alistair MacLean]

David DAICHES was Professor of English at Sussex University and Director of the Institute for Advanced Studies in Humanities at Edinburgh. He has written extensively on Scottish literature and culture. [Robert Fergusson]

Beth DICKSON is a temporary lecturer in the Department of Scottish Literature at Glasgow University and has research interests in early twentieth century Scottish literature. [George Blake; George Douglas Brown; Susan Ferrier; Neil Gunn; John MacDougall Hay; Nan Shepherd]

Islay M. DONALDSON is a freelance writer and researcher who has published a biography of S. R. Crockett as well as volumes on East Lothian and Midlothian gravestones. [S. R. Crockett]

William DONALDSON is a writer, researcher and traditional musician with a particular interest in nineteenth century literature and the popular press. [William Alexander]

Douglas DUNN is a poet and Professor of English at St Andrews University. He has edited anthologies of Scottish poetry and short stories and an edition of Byron's verse. [Lord Byron]

Owen Dudley EDWARDS is Reader in History at Edinburgh University and, in addition to a biography of Conan Doyle, has written on many aspects of Scottish history and culture. [John Buchan; Arthur Conan Doyle]

Jim FERGUSON is a poet and short story writer who has worked as a creative writing tutor and is co-editor of the Neruda Press. [Robert Tannahill]

John A. L. GILFILLAN, originally a teacher of Classics, was, until his retirement, Director of Recreation & Leisure for Midlothian District Council. [Thomas Campbell; Charles Murray]

Valerie GILLIES is a poet, whose recent collection "Running Rock" won a Scottish Arts Council Book Award. She has undertaken research on the work of William Drummond of Hawthornden. [William Drummond]

William GILLIES is Professor of Celtic at Edinburgh University and, among other publications, edited the prose works of Sorley MacLean. [Fionn Mac Colla; James Macpherson]

Rosemary GORING is literary editor and leader writer for "The Scotsman" and has edited a number of literary and other reference works. [James Kennaway; Sidney Goodsir Smith]

Ken HINSHALWOOD was, until his retirement, Local Studies Librarian with Renfrew District Libraries. [William Sharp; James "B. V." Thomson]

Ronald D.S. JACK holds the Chair of Scottish & Medieval Literature at Edinburgh University and has published extensively on early-modern Scottish literature. [Thomas Urquhart]

James MACKAY is a freelance writer whose biographical subjects have included Wallace, Burns, Robert Service and Alexander Graham Bell. [James Barke; Robert Burns]

Rennie McOWAN is a writer and broadcaster with an interest in the Scottish countryside and its literature. Books for children include "Light on Dumyat". [Maurice Walsh]

John MacRITCHIE is a librarian in Kirriemuir, Angus and a regular contributor to professional journals. [J. M. Barrie; Eric Linklater]

Douglas S. MACK is Reader in English Literature at Stirling University and General Editor of the Stirling/South Carolina edition of the works of James Hogg. [James Hogg]

Brian D. OSBORNE is a librarian and writer who has published works on Henry Bell, Neil Munro, Scottish history and the River Clyde. [James Boswell; Neil Munro; Carolina Oliphant]

Chris RAVENHALL is a playwright and lecturer in English studies currently carrying out research on twentieth century Scottish women dramatists. [Joe Corrie; Robert MacLellan]

Alan REID, the Scottish Library Association's Honorary Publications Officer, is Library Services Manager for Midlothian Council. [Henry Mackenzie; Alexander Scott]

David S. ROBB is Senior Lecturer in the Department of English at Dundee University and has written on Muriel Spark and edited the poems of Alexander Scott. [George MacDonald]

James ROBERTSON, a poet and short story writer, was the first holder of the Brownsbank Writing Fellowship. He has edited Miller's work including "My Schools and Schoolmasters". [Hugh Miller]

Mary ROSS formerly lectured at Newbattle Abbey College, where she was the Secretary of the Edwin Muir Society. She now teaches in further and higher education and writes on educational and other subjects. [Edwin Muir]

Trevor ROYLE, author and broadcaster, edited the "Mainstream Companion to Scottish Literature" and has written biographies of literary and military subjects. [R. M. Ballantyne; Compton Mackenzie]

Paul H. SCOTT, a retired diplomat, writes widely on Scottish culture, politics and literature. He is President of the Scottish Centre of PEN International. [John Galt; Robert Garioch]

Iain Crichton SMITH after a career in teaching is now a full time poet, novelist, playwright and short story writer in English and Gaelic. [Alasdair MacMhaighstir Alasdair; Duncan Ban Macintyre]

Louis STOTT worked in adult education and now is a bookseller. He is the author of "Waterfalls of Scotland" and various works of literary topography. [Elizabeth Grant; Andrew Lang; Gavin Maxwell; Tobias Smollet; James Thomson]

John WALKER is a Professor in the Department of Spanish at Queen's University, Ontario who has researched and published extensively on Cunninghame Graham. [Robert Bontine Cunninghame Graham]

Veronica WALLACE is Community Services Librarian with East Lothian Libraries and is involved in the field of local studies provision. [John Home]

Hamish WHYTE is a Senior Librarian in the Mitchell Library Glasgow and edited "Noise and Smoky Breath" a collection of Glasgow poetry. [James Bridie]

Sandy WINTON is Senior Librarian, Technical and Support Services, with Midlothian Libraries. [Allan Ramsay]

Picture acknowledgements

William Alexander	City of Aberdeen Art Gallery and Museums Collections
Joe Corrie	By permission of Morag Corrie
A. J. Cronin	Victor Gollancz
William Drummond	The University of Edinburgh
Jane Duncan	The author's family
Susan Ferrier	From a private collection. reproduced with the permission of the owner
Lewis Grassic Gibbon	The Grassic Gibbon Centre
Neil Gunn	Dairmid Gunn and Alasdair C. Gunn
John MacDougall Hay	Reproduced by kind permission of the Elderslie Kirk Session
Jessie Kesson	Aberdeen Journals Ltd
Sir David Lindsay	The Bodleian Library, University of Oxford (Shelfmark = Gough Scotland 221)
John Gibson Lockhart	Scottish National Portrait Gallery
George MacDonald	University of Aberdeen
Alistair MacLean	Courtesy The Herald & Evening Times
Gavin Maxwell	Galloway Gazette Newspaper Group, Newton Stewart
William Soutar	Perth & Kinross Council Library Service
Maurice Walsh	Rennie McOwan

The illustrations which accompany articles on the following writers were provided by The Trustees of the National Library of Scotland

Marion Angus	Neil Gunn
R. M. Ballantyne	Robert Henryson
John Barbour	Violet Jacob
James Barke	James Kennaway
J. M. Barrie	Andrew Lang
George Blake	Sir David Lindsay
James Bridie	David Lindsay
George Douglas Brown	Eric Linklater
John Buchan	Duncan Ban Macintyre
Catherine Carswell	Sir Compton Mackenzie
Joe Corrie	Ian Maclaren
A. J. Cronin	Robert McLellan
Gavin Douglas	Charles Murray
William Dunbar	Carolina Oliphant
Jane Duncan	Margaret Oliphant
Susan Ferrier	James Thomson ("B.V.")
Elizabeth Grant	Sir Thomas Urquhart

Every effort has been made to seek the permission of copyright holders to reproduce photographs used in this publication.